CLARKE'S
CAMBERLEY AT WAR

(1914-1918)

by

KEN CLARKE

PERSONAL REMINISCENCES
page 1

MOTOR CYCLE CLUB
page 5

EMPIRE DAY
page 6

RAID ON CIRCUS
page 7

LOST AT THE FRONT
page 10

GALLANTRY AWARDS
page 12

ROYAL WEST SURREY REGIMENT
page 14

FRITH HILL CONCENTRATION CAMP
page 15

COURT CASES
page 18

'CAMBERLEY NEWS'
page 20

SCHOOLS
page 25

SUMMARY OF YEARS 1914-1918
page 29

HOUSE OF COMMONS
LONDON SWIA OAA

I warmly congratulate Mr. Ken Clarke on a further excellent book on Camberley. It will prove of great interest, I am sure, to very many people, especially those who have recently moved into the area and would like to know more of its history.

I enthusiastically commend this book and believe it will give many hours of interest and pleasure to all who read it.

Michael Grylls MP

First Edition
ISBN 0 9509945 1 0

© Ken Clarke 1986

Published by KEN CLARKE
24 Heenan Close, Frimley Green, Camberley, Surrey

Designed and printed in England by **ARTWORKS**
Watchmoor Trade Centre, Camberley, Surrey.

(ii)

photos courtesy of Imperial War Museum

London Road, Camberley

photo: 'Camberley News'

"... I recollect once, several of us Camberley boys gathered in a dug-out in the firing line, talking about the old times at home. One of the Company would say 'What about the Carnival?', another saying 'How about going down to the Rec—being early closing day there's sure to be some nice girls for a dance when the band strikes up.' In the middle of these conversations we are brought back to the reality of things by the bursting of a shell close by, or by the Sgt. shouting 'Stand to'. We then have to jump onto the first step and await orders. We are all anxiously looking forward to the end of the war and getting back to the dear old spot again. You may rely upon the Camberley boys to do their best and to keep smiling..."

Private F. Tomms (somewhere in France) 1916
(extract from a letter to the 'Camberley News')

I would like to dedicate this, my second book, to my wife Monica and my children Rebecca and Toby who have, as before, been very understanding about my constant trips to museums and libraries to research.

I would also like to dedicate this book to all those men who lost their lives in the Great War, some of whom I have mentioned in my book.

This book carries on where the first left off, and I look at Camberley during the Great War from 1914 to 1918.

Apart from visiting places to obtain information, I have spoken to a few of Camberley's senior citizens who painted in words for me quite a good picture of what the town was like during this period which I have tried, in some measure, to impart.

I hope you, the reader, will find my second look at Camberley interesting and informative.

Ken Clarke

ONE OF THE MAIN reasons for writing this book, and my previous book (*Clarke's View of Camberley*) was because of my father. I owe a lot to him and his great sense of humour, and to my mother, (also well known for her humour) which I think I must have inherited from them.

I will relate a small tale about my father so that you understand him better.

I was standing in the middle of a large queue in the old Post Office in the London Road when my father came in and on seeing me, came and stood by me. He didn't say a thing, so I said to him "Don't you push in here old man, go to the back of the queue!" He played up to this well and just stood there, with a very humble look on his face. I went on, "I suppose you have come to collect your pension have you? Typical, pushing in front and then just to collect money off us who work for the country." At this stage a middle-aged woman standing in front of me turned round and looked at me most indignantly. My father, who had started to walk to the end of the queue saw this, and thinking she was about to hit me, said "It's all right, he's my son." The woman still looked disgusted with my behaviour though. All good fun, my father loved it—he would.

Back in 1963 while working at Whites Garage, he was asked to write his memories of the firm from when he started there, and I reproduce part of them, just as he wrote them:

"I have been asked to relate my experiences during my 48 years working for Whites Limited. It was April 14th 1914 when I joined the firm, yes, quite a long time ago. My first job was to sweep the front of 42 London Road, under the watchful eye of Mr. P.W. White who told me it had taken me much too long.

My work was to clean sewing machines and gramaphones which soon took me on to fitting new main springs and also governor springs to the gramaphone motors. The repairs to the sewing machines were mostly done by Mr. P.W. White himself with help from his brother.

When Christmas came it kept us very busy, as people came with their gramaphones for us to repair, this being the only means of entertainment as wireless was not with us yet. It would no doubt, be interesting to you that our working hours were 8 to 1, an hour for lunch, and then on to 5 o'clock with half an hour for tea and on Fridays to 7 or 8 o'clock. Saturdays it was somewhere around 10 o'clock. My wages—the grand sum of 2/6d!

I well remember on one Saturday evening being told by Mr. P.W. White to take a cycle after repair, to a house in the Portsmouth Road. The time was about 9.45 in the evening and he kindly told me that I need not come back to the shop (very nice of him).

On most Saturday afternoons my job was to take 6 to 8 two gallon petrol cans on a cycle(!) to Mrs. Langtons, "Kitscroft", Eversley, and bring the empty cans back.

Employees of White's Garage, from left to right: Fred Harvey, Ted Stevenson, Dick Elsigood, Charlie Healey, Ted Dellon, Chris Crowhurst, George Clarke (my father)

PERSONAL REMINISCENCES

My last job on Saturday nights was to clean Mr. and Mrs. White's and their children's shoes. I also cleaned the knives, forks and spoons and chopped enough wood to last the weekend, and all this for 2/6d. a week! But little did Mr. P.W. White know that Mrs. White always gave me a cake and a drink for my services.

Now the business was growing, the cadets at the RMC, as it was then called, were allowed to have motor cycles. Two boys and myself had to keep the motor cycles clean. We had about nine each and the cadets took them out on Wednesday. So on Thursday we started all over again, ready for Saturday. These were inspected by Mr. White and believe me, he often found something wrong with them— what a life!

By this time my wages were 5/6d. Doing quite well now. At about this time, 1915, Whites had a petrol pump installed at 42 London Road. This was a wonderful thing to us, of course. It was worked by hand and I had the job of keeping it clean. It seemed to me that I was the mainstay of Whites in those days, but let me relate, I was the only one who thought so! We had by this time some cars for hire—one an Overland and two Standard 25hp. They were kept very busy taking cadets to London on Wednesdays and Saturdays.

It was always an interesting time when Mr. White was getting ready for motor cycle trials. His machine had a good check over and spares packed. I must tell you he was very successful and won many cups and medals.

Now the First War was well on its way and in early 1917 I was called up and served to the end, and when I got my release I came back to Whites and was put in charge of the Cycle Department which had grown to a large concern. In those days we made our own cycles. My job was making the frames and building the wheels. These cycles were sold at £3.19s.6d. Then the three speeds came into being and it took

My father in the uniform of the Royal Flying Corps, 1917

us quite a time to get to know the working of them, but we won in the end. We also hired cycles out at 6d. an hour as most people could not afford one of their own."

His reminiscences continue right up to the 60s, but I will leave it there in case I write a further book.

My father joined the Royal Flying Corps, which was formed in April 1911, but by April 1918 it merged with the Royal Naval Air Service to form the Royal Air Force, which he joined in the Second World War.

One of the people my father remembers was Mr. Creeper, who was the Lamplighter for Camberley in 1910. He lived in Cross Street. My father saw him many times with his long pole which he poked into the bottom of the lamp and with a hook turned the gas on, lighting the lamp with a wax tape on the top of the pole which was encased to stop it blowing out.

"Bill Dobson, who lived in Princess Street next to Camberley School, was a strange fellow. He used to ride his cycle around the streets with a chicken on the handlebars. It was a pet of his and it never flew away.

Mr. Cudlipp had a forge up at the top of a road by the Brown Jug Public House. Often us kids used to watch him shoeing horses and he also repaired our broken hoops.

Mrs Armstrong, who lived in Princess Street, had her front room turned into a sweet shop where us children spent our half-pennies and pennies. Of course, you got quite a lot for that amount. I have often been into the shop with a farthing to spend.

Two sisters and a brother ran a fish shop in the High Street next to Barclays Bank, (Armstrong or Eighteens). Often I have seen the brother plucking a chicken while it was still alive. He told me that the feathers came out better and did not want so much pulling.

Across the High Street where the pet shop now is, ran a small stream, which ran into a ditch by the railway in Park Street."

Of course not all children had such an ordinary family life and some spent many years in the Royal Albert Orphan Asylum, like Arthur Roser and his brother. Arthur now lives in New Zealand but still writes to me. I mentioned him also in my previous book but I'm including further of his remiscences:

"I can recall quite clearly our woodwork master Mr. Bishop—we called him 'Buster'—a very strict man, robust. One quick look from him was enough to scare the life out of us kids. I remember Stan Cooper's brother, Les, threw a jack plane at him. I'm sure he was not hurt. Cannot remember the punishment. While training at carpentry there I remember the Duke of Connaught giving us an order for a large garden seat in teak. Some 10 to 15 feet long. A great number of mortice and tennon joints had to be worked in this teak, all by hand. It would be interesting to know if it is still around.

My brother Harry took up tailoring. A crippled teacher with very little patience (Mr. Gould) taught him. But he was good and able to train many boys to good advantage. My brother went to Hope Brothers in London on leaving. This firm took several more that I knew."

Another person who was in the Orphanage was Mr. Richard Hawthorn Banister, who was born 22nd March 1903. He was born in London and came to live in Sandhurst. His father died in November 1911 and he entered the orphanage in 1913, possibly through the Vicar of Sandhurst, Randal Parsons. Before this he can remember going on his first train from Sandhurst Halt to Blackwater for 1½d. return and that it cost 1/- to Reading.

He recollects that they were not allowed out, only to fetes and to church parades on Sundays, but about halfway through the First World War, because of the possible threat of air raids, they went to St. Paul's Church instead of marching down to St. Peter's in Frimley. During his time there breakfast and tea consisted of bread and black treacle, with dry currant bread on Sundays. 18 boys to a table who would compete to see who had the most currants in their bread, the record being five. Every morning and night they had a cup of cocoa, except on Sundays, when a mug of tea was given. Apart from church parade on Sundays, there were scripture lessons and a service at the school, bible reading, and then to bed.

His father's mother used to walk from Sandhurst once a month to see him, accompanied by another old lady who would see her nephew. He used to get up at 7, make his bed and the older boys would scrub the dormitories, while the younger ones went to school. There were 18 loaves for 121 boys.

He can remember the meat being sent back to the butchers in Bagshot as unfit for human consumption. They also had soup with 'bits' in it; vegetables? A Mr. Burgess who used to go to the school later became a millionaire and used to send money to the school.

Another time after a spate of thieving there, the two culprits were made to stand in front of the whole school, with the committee also present. Colonel Trench, who was on the committee spoke to one of the boys and asked why he had stolen. "Because I was hungry, sir," was the reply. "What did you have for dinner?" "Two bits of meat and a couple of rotten spuds." The colonel asked, "But didn't you have any blancmange?" The boy said "No sir, I've never had anything like that in my life." That afternoon there were 51 loaves provided as the committee were staying to see the boys fed. Next day it was back to 18 loaves.

When the Duchess of Fife came without warning one Sunday the boys were all put on parade and after she had spoken to each of them she said to Supt. Burn, "These boys are all to have a day's holiday to commemorate my visit." They were given half an hour!

Like me, he has climbed the old clock tower, but while he was up there he hit the bell with a hammer which did not make him the most popular boy at the school. He did not think much of Superintendent Burns or his wife who acted as the matron.

He was a member of the fire brigade which was set up at the school in case of air raids and manned by the senior boys. He can recollect some of the boys and army men setting the common on fire so that they would be called to put it out—just an excuse for getting out of school.

Mr. Trimmer, the shoemaker, had trouble getting the material to make the boys boots, but like all the Trades Masters, they used to teach the trade properly.

On Christmas Day, the Committee would come to the school and serve dinner to the boys—the only day they

got a good meal, he said.

In 1914 he can remember going to a party given by the Duke of Connaught at Bagshot Park and there he saw his first film featuring Fatty Arbuckle and the Keystone Cops. It was, he says, the finest do he had ever been to. He says of the Duke, "He was a smashing old bloke. I spoke to him many times." I bet he would have liked that!

Another senior resident of Camberley who remembers the same period is Miss Edith Emily Todd who was born in London on 6th March 1904, and moved to Camberley in 1909. Her father had a jewellers shop at 5 High Street. He

had three shops there with a bungalow behind. It was all open to Knoll Road, just open fields. A family friend described it as the oasis in the desert. Her father moved from Haslemere to Camberley as it was an up and coming town with the possibility of an opening for a jewellers shop. Camberley was full of interesting people in those days, including Lady Berkeley who had two daughters, and lots of major generals.

She remembers Frederic Robinson the photographer in the High Street and all the beautiful photos that were on display in his window. Unfortunately when he died all his material was destroyed.

Some of the earliest people to have cars she thinks were the doctors in the town. There was also a horse drawn bus service between Camberley and Blackwater railway stations.

During the First World War all the curtains had to be well drawn at night. On Armistice Day she was at school in Farnham and at 10.45 they had their normal mid-morning recess. It seemed to last a long time and then she recollects hearing the church bells ringing. It must have been about 12 midday before they were all called in and the headmistress announced that the war had ended. They were then given the rest of the day off. Everyone was so overjoyed and spent the time visiting the tea shops and cycling around the town.

She also remembers the water carts laying the dust in the summer, bread costing 4½d. a loaf, and granulated sugar 1½d. a pound. On Saturdays bananas would be 6d. for eight as they would not keep for the weekend. About 1917 a man, who she thinks was a Mr. Holmes, used to drive a cart from Chobham selling fruit and vegetables at 1½d. for a pound of apples or plums. 40 oranges could be had for 1/-.

She remembers all the big houses which have now been sold off, and many houses replacing one large house. She also knew Captain Robert Haining as he was then before his promotion. Hence the school named after him at Mytchett.

Camberley Railway Station was a bustling little place with the Station Master very smart in his peaked cap, lots of people, and children on their way to school. There were booking offices on both sides of the platforms.

She proved to be a very good talker and what I thought was only going to be a short visit, proved to take the whole afternoon. But I am very grateful to her and to all the other people who have taken the time and trouble to talk to me about life in Camberley in those far off days when life was so very different and, I believe, taken at a slower pace than it is these days.

MISS PROLE'S SERVANTS AGENCY

In a 1913 Street Directory the shop is described as a fancy repository, (that is a place where valuables are deposited for safety) and was situated at 17 High Street, Camberley.

Mrs. Ivy Potten describes her as a "tall, majestic figure with an awesome bust".

She used to find suitable servants for the gentry in Camberley, and situations for those looking for work in service.

She also sold articles made by patients in Brookwood Hospital.

Camberley Railway Station

London Road, Yorktown, Camberley

Frimley Road, Yorktown, Camberley

Park Street, Camberley

MOTOR CYCLE CLUB

IN APRIL 1914, four months before the outbreak of war, life was still quite normal, and the Camberley Motor Cycle Club was no exception to that rule. It was in that month that they had their opening run of the year to Salisbury, the home of the Captain of the Club, (Mr. E. Collins) who very kindly offered the members an invitation to lunch.

On the run down to Salisbury the members had a reliability trial for prizes, kindly donated by Mr. P.W. White, the founder of Whites Garage, where my father worked for 65 years.

All the members met at 8.45am and after a photograph was taken, a start was made. Mr. E.E. Collins in his motor car, accompanied by his wife, was first away at 9 am.

The members who were competing in the reliability trial followed at intervals of one minute between each. The competitors were in order of getting away. A.H. Ninnis (Hon Sec), C. Knowles, G. Sparvell, Cranham, Elmer, J. Way (Sidecar), Norris, B.D. Crooks, W. Vaughan, W. Hedges, A. Pickard, Watson, Shaw, H.P. Butler, Wilfred B. Styer (President of the Club), P. Holloway, Mr. Stevens (Sidecar). Mr. White took a party in his motor car.

The distance from Camberley to Salisbury is 52 miles, and this was covered in a reliability run to time at an average speed of 20 miles per hour. The first competitor being scheduled to leave Camberley at 9am and to reach Salisbury at 12.06. This was allowing for stops of 15 minutes at Basingstoke and Andover. In addition to being checked at the above places there was a secret check between Whitchurch and Andover carried out by E.E. Collins, P. W. White and H.A. Jamieson. On the first section from Camberley to Basingstoke, Mr. Vaughan did best and was only 15 seconds out on his scheduled time.

In the next section from Basingstoke to the secret check, four miles on from Whitchurch, Mr. Sparvell did best and was within five seconds of his scheduled time. At the Andover check point, four of the competitors arrived exactly on their respective times. They were Mr. Ninnis, Mr. Crooks, Mr. Vaughan and Mr. Shaw. Mr. Cranham was only five seconds out.

At Salisbury, Mr. Sparvell was the best, five seconds out, while Mr. Ninnis was 15 seconds out.

On the way there were only five missing; one of them had trouble with his machine and the others including the President stayed behind to render assistance. However, they all arrived in time to enjoy their lunch.

The result of the trial reliabilty run was:

	Min/sec.		Min/sec.		Min/sec.
Mr. Sparvell	1.21	Mr. Vaughan	3.00	Mr. Hedges	5.13
Mr. Cranham	1.31	Mr. Pickard	3.22	Mr. Elmer	5.59
Mr. Crooks	1.43	Mr. Ninnis	3.25	Mr. Way	7.30
Mr. Watson	3.43	Mr. Knowles	4.15	Mr. Norris	13.27

At Salisbury the Club took an excellent luncheon arranged by Mr. Collins, with more than 30 people present.

After the meal the speeches were fully reported and make interesting reading now, some 72 years later. Mr. Hedges started the speeches off by saying that it was his pleasant duty to propose "Success to the Camberley Motor Cycling Club and as Chairman of the Committee, to express their thanks to Mr. Collins for his kind hospitality to them. (Applause). They had had a very enjoyable run down to Salisbury, the run over the Downs being very fine."

After the speeches, the prize-giving commenced. Mr. Sparvell who came first, received a motor cycle horn, and Mr. Cranham in second place received a handle bar watch. The members then heard from Mr. Ninnis that it was hoped to have another trial in about a month's time and that the Club had also been invited to lend their support to the Camberley Carnival on July 19th by sending two representatives to the Carnival Committee. The members agreed to send Mr. Collins and Mr. Ninnis.

The club remained in Salisbury until 3.30pm and at the suggestion of Mr. Collins, had a fine run of 10 miles over the Wiltshire Downs to see the Druidical Temple at Stonehenge, and then on to Amesbury where they had tea before heading homewards via Bulford Camp, Weyhill, Andover and Basingstoke.

They reached Camberley between 8pm and 9pm after a most enjoyable day's outing.

What a joy it must have been to go on these outings in the first years of the motor vehicle, although the condition of the roads must have been poor in comparison to roads of today.

THE 22nd MAY was celebrated each year in schools as Empire Day. When I was at school I can well remember wearing my cub uniform for the occasion. (I had nice knees in those days!).

Before the Great War the children would normally be addressed by some colonel on the importance of the Empire and there would be prizes for the best essay on the subject. Admiral Johnstone used to visit one of the schools on this day quite regularly. In the afternoon London Road Recreation Ground would ring to the squeals and shouts of children enjoying the arranged games and sitting down to a tea served up by many volunteers, including some of their teachers.

A great ceremony was the raising of the Flag and this continued to take place throughout the war, usually accompanied by the singing of the National Anthem and the hymn, "O God our help in Ages Past".

The War put a stop to the other celebrations and the Rec. remained silent on those days until hostilities ceased.

Children were made to feel that the Empire was important and something to be proud of, and why not? The recent conflict in the Falkland showed, in my opinion, that when it comes to the crunch the vast majority of us are still proud to be British, as the welcome home for the *Canberra* and the *Queen Elizabeth II* showed.

Many senior residents to whom I have spoken, remember Empire Days well, and how much they were enjoyed until their postponement.

I think the photographs (taken a year before the outbreak of War) show what really went on, not only for the children but also for the Old Crimean War Veterans—what tales they must have told the children about their experiences of war.

Of course, when Empire Day was resumed after the War, it could never be quite the same again.

EMPIRE DAY

Empire Day Celebrations at Camberley Recreation Ground:
Top left hand corner: Crimean War Veterans
Above: Boys removing their shoes in preparation for a contest
Below: Girls' races

All photographs on this page courtesy of Surrey Heath Museum

IT WAS NOT OFTEN a travelling circus visited Camberley but in September 1916 one pitched on land fronting the Frimley Road, belonging to Mr. George Doman. Anyone who attended the performance on this particular Monday would have talked about it for years afterwards.

Colonel Ponsonby Watts the local recruiting officer and other military representatives, knowing that visiting circus were always well patronised, decided to have a great round up with a view to 'capturing' eligible men who had not yet reported themselves for service. He arranged the raid with Police Sergeant Kenward and members of the Special Constabulary, plus the Camberley and Yorktown platoon of the Volunteer Training Corps.

The performance commenced at 8pm and the tent was crowded, probably containing between three and four thousand people. Between 8pm and 9pm the police and special constables, according to instructions, waited in Woodland Road, whilst Col. Watts and Sgt. Kenward went to the circus and notified the proprietors of what they intended to do.

Sgt. Kenward then went to the Drill Hall where The Volunteer Training Corps were being drilled, and with the platoon commander's consent, marched the platoon to Woodland Road to join the police.

Arriving at the circus, the police and volunteers secured the exits to make sure no man of military age left the tent and then Colonel Watts and Sergeant Kenward entered the ring. Colonel Ponsonby Watts then informed the audience that he and those with him were there for the purpose of examining the papers and documents of men of military age, and added that what was being done was in the name of the King—an announcement that was greeted with applause.

Sgt. Kenward then requested that all men of military age enter the ring. A great many did and an examination of their papers commenced, whilst the details of those who did not have the necessary papers were taken. There were of course, a number of 'shy' gentlemen who did not believe in putting themselves forward who stayed in their seats.

One local man left by going out under the canvas side of the tent, only to be promptly grabbed by three members of the Volunteer Training Corps. One of the female performers, dressed in male attire for her act, asked "Do you want me? I am of military age and wear the breeches."

Suddenly all the lights in the tent went out, leaving the place in utter darkness. Women were shrieking and children started to cry. The police tried to calm the people down and luckily nothing untoward happened to anybody, although one of the constables, P.C. Reed, found himself in an uncomfortable position. Having been put in charge of one of the exits to prevent people leaving, he suddenly found three performing horses behind him, evidently anxious to enter the ring to perform. However, in the true

RAID ON CIRCUS

tradition of the police, he managed to prevent the horses from getting past him.

The circus tent was illuminated for the performance by acetylene gas jets, supplied from a generator at the foot of the centre tent pole. Those who were present were of the opinion that the gas had been shut off deliberately by a man who perhaps had no papers to show and did not want to answer embarrassing questions.

As if that was not enough for one night, worse was to follow when a match was thrown into the generator, which immediately started to burn. This was quickly extinguished but it was not possible to relight the gas jets. The proprietors provided a hurricane hand-lamp, but the inspection of papers and the circus performance had to be abandoned.

The possibility of panic however still remained, but Sgt. Kenward rose to the occasion and averted this. He thanked the audience for the great forebearance they had shown, for the coolness with which they had behaved, and for the keeness with which they had assisted. He reminded them that the action taken was a matter of national duty. Then he did what any 'showman' would have done: he invited them to join him in singing the National Anthem, which, they did, heartily. The audience then left, no doubt to talk about the evening for many a week to come. Well, wouldn't you?.

It had the desired effect though, for up to Tuesday evening, Colonel Watts had the names of 60 lads under the age of 18 who said they would attest in the new B Group which had just been created.

That's one way to get 'volunteers'!

F.W. Abbot Anderson
Lt. Col. KOR Lancaster Reg.

W.C. Allen
R.M.A.

E.A. Allen
Log Stoker RN

G. Alexander
Manchester Reg.

W. Andress
London Reg.

G. Apps
Border Reg.

E. Attewell
R.W. Surrey.

W.E.C. Atkinson
Capt. Cornwall L.I.

C.J.J. Baker
R.C.A.

H.L. Chenevix Baldwin
Capt 58th Rifles F.F. Indian Army.

W.S. Bannatyne
Lt. Col. Kings Liverpool Reg.

A. Barrett
R.W. Surrey

L. Barrett
16th Lancers.

E.W. Bartlett
Canadian Engineers.

H. Beavan
Rifle Brigade.

F. Bedbrook
Lt. Cpl. R.W. Surrey.

F.C.F. Biscoe
Capt. Worc Reg.

R. Boileau
Colonel R.E.

F.H. Bond
2nd Lt. R.F.A.

C. Bracknell
51st Australians Inf.

J.D.D. Brancker
Major D.S.O., R.C.A.

H.F. Brazier
Royal Engineers.

J. Brewer
R.W. Surrey.

W. Brooks
N. Staffordshire.

F.C. Brooks
2nd Lt. R.F.A.

A.W. Bryan
Canadian Infantry.

L. Budd
Sgt. Machine Gun Guards.

S.L. Budd
Sgt. Kings Reg. Lancaster Reg.

H.G. Burdett
Capt. Westminster Dragoons.

J. Bunyan
46th Canadian Inf.

A.B. Cadell
2nd Lt. Devon Reg.

F.W. Callingham
R.W. Surrey.

D. Campbell
Sgt. D.C.M., R.F.A.

E.C. Capner
R.W. Kent.

H.H. Carney
Sgt. Lein Reg.

L.C. Chambers
N. Staff Reg.

A.A.M. Charles
Capt. R.F.A.

A.G. Cheshire
15th Hussars.

C.C. Chesney
Lt. 117th Mahrattas.

G.T. Church
Sgt. Maj. R.E.

A. Clarkson
Sgt. K.O.R. Lancaster Reg.

C.W. Cleeve
R.W. Surrey.

F.T. Clough
Cpl. R.W. Kent.

G.W.C. Coe
R. Berks Reg.

C.A.J. Coe
R.W. Surrey.

F.J. Clarke
M.M., R.W. Surrey.

H. Cook
R.W. Surrey.

C.W. Cook
Sgt. R.A.S.C.

A.E. Cook
R.W. Surrey.

J.H. Cook
R.W. Surrey.

A.R. Cooper
L/Cpl. R.W. Surrey.

G. Collins
R.A.S.C.

F.C. Coles
Machine Cun Corps.

A. Coleman
R.W. Surrey.

W. Coombes
R.A.S.C.

G. Compton
London Reg.

O. Colegate
Australian Imp. Forces

V. Colegate
Australian Imp. Forces

T. Collyer
Sgt. E. Yorks Reg.

F.C. Comer
R.W. Kent.

S.J. Conduit
London Rifle Brigade.

J.H. Cox
E. York Reg.

F. Cracknell
Royal Navy.

V.E.B. Cunningham
Artists Rifles

R.A.N. Currie
Brig. Gen. C.M.C., D.S.O.
Somerset L.I.

J.A. Dale
Royal Fusiliers.

J.E. Dale
R.N.D.

H.J. Davis
Royal Navy.

S. Davis
Royal Navy.

J.C. Day
Royal Fusiliers.

W.H. Day
D.C.M., R.W. Surrey.

F.C. Dean
R.W. Surrey.

T. Dewey
Hants Reg.

N.P. Dowding
Sgt. RM-LI

J.H. Drake
L/Cpl Yorks & Lancs Reg.

A. Draper
Machine Gun Guards.

W. Draper
R.W. Surrey.

A.J.B. Eddenden
Sgt. Military Foot Police

H.B. Edgell
R.W. Surrey.

A.J.B. Ellis
R.W. Surrey.

F.J.H. Ellis
L/Cpl R. Berks Reg.

C.A. Elmer
Royal Air Force.

A.W. Elsley
R.W. Surrey.

V.E. Emmings
R. Berks Reg.

H. Cope Evans
2nd Lt. D.S.O., R.A.F.

A.W. Faggetter
R.W. Surrey.

N.D. Findlay
Brig. Gen. C.B., R.A.

C.C. Ford
Capt. Somerset L.I.

T. Brittain Forward
Capt. KOR Lancaster Reg.

J.D. Fowler
Lt. 16th Lancers.

F.G. Frankum
Machine Gun Guards.

E.E. Fuller
Hants Reg.

E.W. Furse
Lt. Col. R.F.

F.M. Gillespie
Lt. Col. South Wales Borderers.

W.T. Gillett
Devon Reg.

W. Goatley
RND.

A.J.V. Goddard
R.W. Surrey

A.E. Goddard
L/Cpl R. Fusiliers.

H.E. Goddard
Middlesex Reg.

A.H. Godwin
L/Cpl R Berks Reg.

H. Godwin
R.W. Surrey.

F.M. Godwin
R.W. Surrey.

S.A. Goldsmed
2nd Lt. Worc Reg.

A.M. Graham
Capt. 5th Gurkha Rifles.

G.H. Hall
Sgt. R.W. Surrey.

F.D. Hall
Cpl. R.W. Surrey.

P.R. Hall
Hants Reg.

W.J. Hall
Cpl Middlesex Reg.

S.W. Hammond
Sgt. MM., R. Berks Reg.

E.A. Hampton
R.W. Surrey.

F.J. Handford
R. Inns. Fusiliers.

A.A. Handford
Rifle Brigade.

A. Hanks
R.W. Surrey.

A.J.V. Harden
2nd Lt. R. Sussex Reg.

R.G. Harrington
2nd Dragoon Guards.

C.R. Harrison
Cpl R.W. Surrey.

W.G. Harrison
R.W. Surrey.

G.H. Henty
Major, Suffolk Reg.

H. Herrington
Royal Navy.

W.C. Hiles
L/Sgt. Grenadier Guards.

A.E. Holdaway
Sergeant, KRRC.

J.H.B. Hollings
Lt. 21st Lancers.

A.C.E. Howes
Hants Reg.

C.E. Hunt
Capt. MC, 34th Sikh Pioneers

A. Inglis
Hants Reg.

O.W. Jackman
2nd Lt. M.M., R.W. Surrey.

V.S. Jackman
R.W. Surrey

G.J. Jones
L/Cpl South Wales Borderers

A. Kyberd
Sgt. RASC.

F.R. Lacey
R.H.A.

T. Lacey
R.C.A.

J. Larkin
Sgt. Canadian Forces.

E. Ledger
Can. Cameron Highlanders.

P.C. Eliott Lockhart
Col., Scinde Rifles FF.

R.C. Longhurst
Queen Victoria Rifles.

D. Macbean
Capt. Gordon Highlanders.

F.J. Mace
Cpl. East African MT Corps.

C. Mackenzie
Lt. Seaforth Highlanders.

D.S. Macinnes
Brig. Gen. C.M.C., D.S.O., R.E.

B.H.B. Magrath
Major, E. Lancs Reg.

H. Marshallsea
R. Berks Reg.

H. Martin
Machine Gun Corps.

J.R. Martin
R.A.S.C..

J.W. Martin
R. Berks Reg.

C. Masters
Royal Navy.

L. Masters
Leics Reg.

R.J. Mathias
Sgt. Royal Engineers.

W.T. Mathias
Sgt. RAMC.

M. Mills
R. Berks Reg.

S.D. Miller
2nd Lt. R. Innis Fusiliers.

G.B. Mayne
Major, CIH.

J.M. Mayne
2nd Lt. R.F.A.

V.C. Mayne
Lt. South Wales Borderers.

H. Moth
E. Surrey Reg.

W.G. Mullard
L/Cpl Post Office Rifles.

A. Mustow
Hants Reg.

F.H. Neville
K. Shropshire L.I.

G.D.A. Newman
Northampton Reg.

J. Nicklinson
Grenadier Guards.

W. North
Hants Reg.

A.G. Nunn
R.A.S.C.

J. Nunn
Sgt. Major, D.C.M., MM., Hants Reg.

O.G. Oliver
Cpl. R.A.S.C.

J.B. Orr
Major, DSO, Norfolk Reg.

G.W. Over
L/Cpl. R.W. Surrey.

Edward D. Pain
Capt. Somerset L.I.

S.J. Parsons
Cpl. MM., R.W. Surrey.

H. Parker
Cpl., R.W. Surrey.

G.W. Pawley
Seaman Gunner, RN.

G.E. Penhallow
KOR Lancaster Reg.

C.O.L. Penrose
Major, MC., R.C.A..

H.P. Philby
Major, D.S.O., Yorks & Lancs Reg.

D.D. Philby
Lt., D.S.O., R. Dubin Fus.

P.Plume
R.A.S.C.

S.G.H. Pobgee
Cpl. 16th Lancers.

A. Poulter
Leic. Reg.

H. Poulter
London Reg.

G. Poulter
Hants Reg.

F. Prentice
London Reg.

C.A. Proudfoot
Capt. 53rd Sikhs FF.

J.W. Randall
Middx. Reg.

E.H. Reid
Capt. Suffolk Reg.

A. Rose
Royal Navy.

B.G. Rugg
Post Office Rifles.

A.G. Rumble
Bedford Reg.

A.G. Rush
Sgt. Essex Reg.

E. Rust
BOR R.H.A.

C. Ryley
Major, R.A.M.C.

A.H. Saunders
Lt., R. Berks Reg.

A.E. Scott
2nd Lt. Rifle Brigade.

W. Shakespeare
Coldstream Guards.

F.L. Sharp
Col., R.F.A..

F.H. Sharp
Lt., R.F.A.

W.J. Sheahan
GM Sgt. Hants Reg.

H. Skinner
Rifle Brigade.

C. Shortt
KO Shropshire L.I.

J. Sillick
R.A.S.C.

C.G. Smallbones
Sgt., R.W. Surrey Reg.

S.W. Smith
Sgt., R.W. Surrey Reg.

M.C.A. Spong
Sgt. R.A.F.

W.C. Stone
2nd Lt. R. Munster Fusiliers.

W.H. Steed
L/Cpl. Hants Reg.

A.E. Steer
Royal Fusiliers.

F.J.L. Stokes
L/Sgt. R.W. Surrey Reg.

J. Street
N. Staff Reg.

G.S. Styles
R.W. Surrey.

A.D. Talbot
Capt. Lancs Fusiliers.

F.G.B. Thomas
Lt., Essex Reg.

W. Thomas
Canadian Forces.

A.R. Treherne
2nd Lt., R. Berks.

F.M. Chenevix Trench
Major, R.F.A.

F.G. Tripp
Sgt. R.W. Surrey.

S. Trussler
R.W. Surrey.

A. Tyrell
Sgt. MM R.W. Surrey

G. Tyrell
Sgt. London Irish Rifles.

B. Ussher
Capt. Lein Reg.

F.N. Verran
Lt. Wilts Reg.

R. Vyse
Sgt. R.H.A.

C. Walker
R.F.A.

G.A. Webb
R.W. Surrey.

A. Wellman
R.W. Surrey.

E.N. Wells
Northampton Reg.

C.R.J. West
Sgt. R.W. Kent

J. Williams
R. Welsh Fusiliers.

F.C. Woods
Lt. R.W. Surrey.

S. Woodley
Nov Scotia Reg.

A.J. Wye
R.W. Surrey.

F. Yarde
Sgt., Coldstream Guards.

E.E. Yates
KOYLI

A. Young
Sgt., R.W. Surrey.

F.W. Goddard
Royal Engineers

W.H. Pennington
12th Cavalry Major Indian Army.

A.P.A. Elphinstone
Lt. Col. (IA) 3rd Tyneside Scottish.

In addition to the names on the War Memorial there is also a list in the St. Tarcisius Roman Catholic Church. Some of them are listed on the War Memorial.

T. Brennan
L/Cpl., R.W. Surrey.

A. Brennan
L/Cpl., Hants.

G. Coleman
Sgt. Worcester.

R.F. Gibson
Pte., Royal Engineers.

J.S. Gibson
Pte., Guernsey Rifles.

L.G. Jones
L/Cpl. K.O. Lancs.

A.P. McCabe
Lt. Surrey.

R. Mannering
Pte., Hants.

J. Sillenec
Pte., Hants.

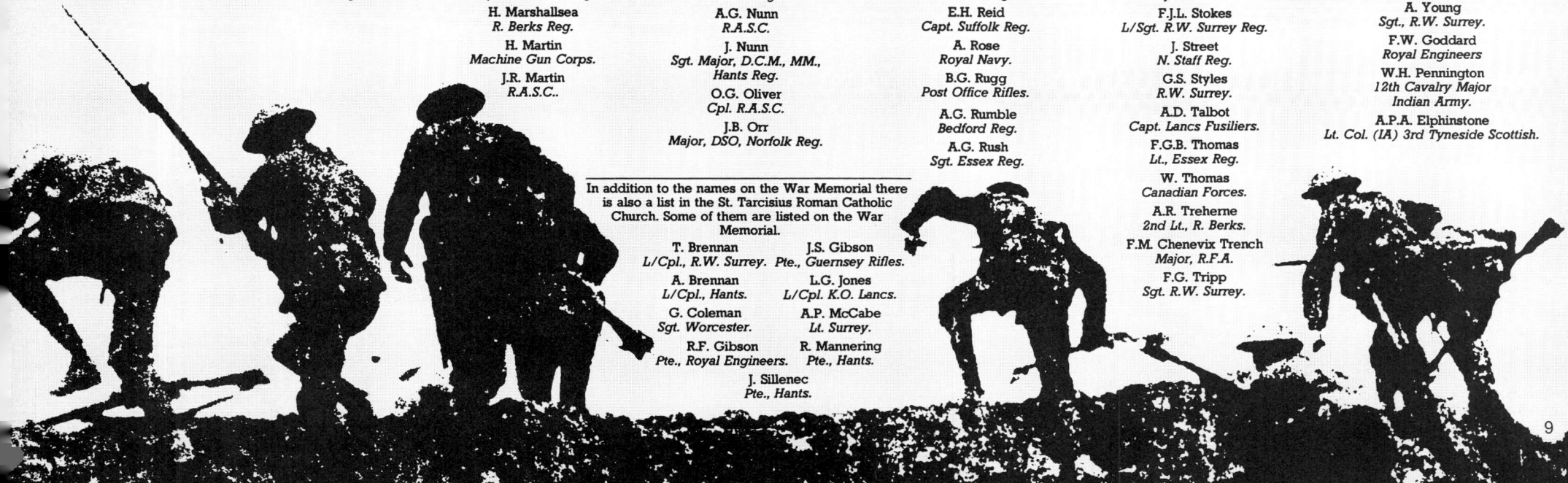

WHILST RESEARCHING for this chapter, I could not help but be saddened by the loss of so many local men (many who were members of local football teams). Hardly a week went by without a local man reported missing or dead.

Most people in Camberley know where the war memorial stands. But how many people know anything of the lives and deaths of those listed on it, particularly those men who lost their lives in the Great War, almost 70 years ago? I have found out, from the newspaper accounts of the time and from war records, about some of the men whom I feel are typical of the husbands, sons, fathers and brothers who lost their lives fighting for their country and I found the letters written to the bereaved families, notifying them of the death of their loved ones, poignant reminders of what those who stayed behind had to bear during that period.

On 17th April 1915 the death was announced of an old Camberley Council schoolboy, **Sgt. Harry Carney** of the 1st Leinster Regiment whose parents lived in the Frimley Road. He had served three years in India and had returned to the British Expeditionary Force. *"He was a bright young fellow of 26, keen in all his military duty and loved by his many friends to whom his loss will bring much sorrow."* He was killed on 15th March at St. Eloi whilst leading his platoon after the officer had been killed.

Sgt. John Larkin, who had previously been reported missing was now reported dead. His wife who resided at 1 Cromwell Road received a telegram from the Canadian Record Office. He was serving with the 10th Canadian Battalion and had died in France on 5th June 1915. The *Camberley News* made a great play on the fact that Mr. Larkin was 52 when he joined up while living in Canada and hoped this would have a good effect on those who had not yet enlisted.*"If any shirkers with an ounce of patriotism left in them read this, we should imagine that Col. Ponsonby Watts and his staff at the recruiting office will have a busy time during the next few days."* He was 54 when he died, and the father of four children. He had served 18 years with the *Royal Irish Fusiliers and 16 years with the Royal Military and Staff Colleges.*

At the beginning of January 1916 the death was announced of **Sgt. Sidney Smith** of the Royal West Surrey Regiment who was one of three brothers and lived in Cross Street, Camberley. His mother received a letter from his C.O. GHH Scott OC C Company written 5th January in the trenches. *"It is with the most heartfelt regret that I have to write to tell you bad news. It is about Sgt. Smith in my Company. The Germans shelled us with trench mortar bombs yesterday and the dug out in which your son and another man were sitting was destroyed. Both of them must have been instantly killed as they were buried deep under the debris, and had obviously never known anything. This morning we buried the Sgt. The Colonel, Adjutant and many other officers were there, also many of his platoon and*

LOST AT THE FRONT

representatives of all the other platoons. I do not think there is anything more to say except again to tell you that your grief is shared by everyone who knew him, believe me."

On 26th February notification was given of the death of **Lt. Ashton B. Cadell** son of Dr. Cadell of "Foxlease" Camberley. He died of wounds received at the front whilst serving with the Royal West Kent Regiment. *"This gallant young officer had studied with Mr. Tinniswood at Holmesdale, Camberley and was very popular."* He had received his commission with the Devon Regiment.

On 10th June as a result of the Battle of Jutland **George W. Pawley** 24 years, 1st class gunner, lost his life while on the "Black Prince". He was the eldest son of Mr. and Mrs. Pawley of the "Fox and Hounds" at Yorktown. He joined the navy as a boy. Lost on the same ship was **Herbert Herrington** 23 years who came from Frimley Green. **Lord Kitchener** died during the same battle on the ship the "Hampshire".

September 2nd 1916 saw the announcement of the death of **Captain Edward Day Pain** aged 36 years of the Somerset Light Infantry, the eldest son of Alderman Arthur C. Pain J.P. of St. Catherines, Frimley,. After studying engineering he then became a journalist on the staff of the *Northern Mail* and then came to work in London. He joined the first public school's battalion of the Royal Fusiliers, finally obtaining his commission in the Somerset Light Infantry in December 1914. He had been mentioned in orders for the plucky part he played in gathering information on a night operation. His father received the details of his death in a letter from Lt. Col. T.F. Ritchie (Somerset L.I.) *"I greatly regret having to inform you that your son was killed while consolidating a newly captured trench, captured on the 18th August. Up to the time of his death he had led his Company with great skill and courage. I looked upon your son as one of my most valuable officers, one upon whose judgement and character I could always rely and he possessed a charming personality which made him a delightful companion. Owing to the number of wounded to be cleared it was impossible to bring his body back so he was buried beside the German trench he had so gallantly captured. This point is about 400 yards south east of north east corner of Delville Wood and 50 yards north of the Longueval to Ginchy Road. With much sympathy from us all…"*

In October 1916 the death of **Sgt. Charles Reginald Jack West** was reported, He had fallen in action on 7th October. He was a regular member of St. Georges Choir and there was a special service for him on Sunday 14 June 1919 and a

---

beautiful six foot floral cross made up of pure white flowers, was placed facing the choir stalls. The card attached to it read *"Sacred to the memory of Sgt. Charles Reginald Jack West who fell in action in France, October 7th 1916 aged 21 years.".*

Two months later a fellow chorister was also killed, **Private Charles Coe** aged 19 years. At the following Sunday service the vicar, the Rev. F.N. Kingdom offered his and the congregation's sympathy to the family of the late soldier who had volunteered for the bombing party in which he was killed. He ended up with the words *"Greater love hath no man than this that a man lay down his life for his friends."*

On 27th January 1917 the news of the death of **Private F.H. Neville** of the Shropshire Light Infantry was received. He was 24 years old, and had been born in Camberley and attended Yorktown School. He lived at 1 York Terrace, Frimley Road, was married and had three children. Before the war he worked as a doorman at the Staff College. He was killed by an exploding bomb, which also killed an officer.

On 14th April 1917 the death was announced of **Lt. Frank C. Woods** son of the late Surgeon Major Woods of Bath Road, Camberley. He had been killed during an attack on the railway station at Croisseles in France when his battalion came under heavy German machine gun fire. He had only just returned to the front after having had three operations and it was doubtful that he was fully fit but he pressed his claim and was successful in being allowed to rejoin his regiment. He was 29 years old and a member of St. Georges Choir.

In May 1917 **L/Cpl W.G. Mullard** was killed in France while serving with the Post Office Rifles of the London Regiment. He was shot through the head by a German sniper while his battalion were consolidating a position they had gained. He joined the Post Office as a messenger in 1897 and became a postman in 1901. He joined the Post Office Rifles in 1915 and had been in France for about 12 months. His home was in Victoria Road, Camberley and he left a wife and three children, the youngest of whom at 3 months he never saw. Before the war he was a well known football player, having played for St. George's team, and was also a regular member of the Post Office team.

At this time the Post Office announced that six of their numbers had been killed in the war. Among them was **Rifleman Bertrum G. Rugg,** who on 25th August 1916 was presumed dead, having been reported missing since 7th October. He lived at 4 Alexander Road, Camberley. He was also a member of the Post Office Football team. He was buried in Warlencourt British Cemetery in France.

At the end of October 1916 **Private F.A. Parker** of the same regiment had a lucky escape. He was wounded and was recovering in a hospital in Camberley. He had joined with two other postmen, **T. Milton** and **B.G. Rugg.** The last he saw of them was Milton with his hands apparently clutching his side and Rugg endeavouring to hold him up. Since then nothing had been heard of them. Parker went on with the advance and was badly wounded in the knee. He fell and crawled to a shell hole where he stayed for eight days before being found. The hole was in Noman's land with shells from both sides whizzing over him and he had to hide by day. When he fell he only had his rations and at night time he had to crawl to other fallen soldiers and use their rations and water to survive. On the eighth day he heard voices and decided to take his chance. On trying to shout he found his voice had gone but he was fortunate that they were colonial soldiers who took him to hospital.

In May 1917 it was confirmed that **Private Milton** was a prisoner of war. He was released from Germany in 1919, having spent six months in a German hospital at a POW camp in north east Germany where he suffered much hardship which was felt to have attributed to his early death on 24th January 1929 at the age of 42. He lived at 12 Moorlands Road, Camberley, and left a wife and daughter.

On 15th June 1918 notification of the death of **Trumpeter Alfred George Cheshire** was received by his parents who lived at 3 Burford Road, Camberley who at 18 was the youngest of three sons. He had joined his father's old regiment the 15th Hussars and was killed in the heavy fighting in France. A letter from one of his colleagues was sent to his family. *"... He, together with six more of a party were sent out at dawn to reinforce a part of the line that had been reported by our officers to be a weak salient. It was while in the open that we unfortunately came under observation from a Bosch machine gun which accounted for four other fellows. Captain Arnett (killed later that day) and I managed to get your son under cover of the trench and although every endeavour was made to keep life going, we failed and your son died a short while after being hit. His last words to my knowledge were 'mother, mother'. One consolation, if consolation it can be called, was that he died peacefully and without any pain or disfigurement. It was not until darkness set in that I buried him just over from where he had been killed. Ever since the offensive commenced I had your son alongside of me and to be so young was a credit to his regiment, knowing no fear, resourceful and tactful in critical moments and it affected me more than I like to admit when he got killed. His death left me practically without a pal, more so when I found myself the only survivor."* What a very thoughtful letter which no doubt helped his family at the time.

On 21st September 1918 the death was announced of **Rifleman George Compton,** Post Office Rifles who had previously been reported missing. He died in France, aged 31 years and left a widow and two small children. He had joined his regiment in 1917.

On 23rd November, 12 days after the end of the war, the death was announced of **Sapper H.F. Brazier** of "Graitney Lodge West", Camberley. He died on 17th September in Darmstadt as a prisoner of war. He was with the Royal Engineers and had been a Sunday School pupil and chorister at St. Paul's Church. It was his third time in France, having been wounded on two earlier occasions. In a letter to his home the officer had said, *"In all he did he showed himself a true Briton."*

When I see the Armistice Day Remembrance Service at the Albert Hall, I can quite understand why people want it to be continued, and why not? Millions of lives were lost and it is the least we who were left or came after can do as a mark of respect to the fallen.

TIDINGS WANTED

Private Patrick J. O'Donnell

We are asked, on behalf of the relatives of the undermentioned soldier, to appeal to any of our readers for news of No. 2111 Private Patrick J. O'Donnell, C Company, 1st/4th Royal Sussex Regiment, 160th Brigade, 53rd Welsh Division, Mediterranean Expeditionary Force. He was reported missing at the Dardanelles on 17th August, 1915. Any information will be glady received by his mother, Mrs. O'Donnell, 53, York-road, Aldershot.

THE ROLL OF HONOUR
Lieut. A.E. Scott

Nearly a year ago we recorded, with an appreciative paragraph, the gaining of a commission by the son of Mr. and Mrs. H. Scott, of Princess-street, Camberley. After long service with the Sherwood Foresters, in which he saw much hard fighting Lieutenant Arthur E. Scott was gazetted to the Rifle Brigade in July of last year. Soon after he was sent to France and in October was slightly wounded while on patrol, but continued to serve with the regiment until January 14th last, when he came home on leave. He again returned to France and, after taking a six weeks' special course, rejoined his regiment on March 19th.

We greatly regret to say that only two days later, in the great enemy offensive, the splendid young officer was killed. He leaves a widow and child to mourn his loss, and his bright, happy spirit, his cheery optimism, will long be missed by his many friends.

Writing to Mrs. Scott, the Chaplain to the Battalion (the Rev. H.R.S. Tringham, C.F.), says: "Dear Mrs. Scott—You will have heard from the War Office the very sad news of your brave husband's death. I have made enquiries and find that he was killed on the first day of the battle while in command of Dean Trench. The Colonel would have written before, but he and the Battalion have been fighting continuously until the last few days. He wishes me to tell you that he has lost a very valuable officer. Your dear husband was always cheerful and uncomplaining under the most trying circumstances and helped to hearten his men by his own courage and seeming indifference to danger. As far as I can make out he was killed by a shell which killed him instantly. He and his men defended the position given him to hold until all fell. The Colonel and the Battalion wish me to express their deep sympathy with you in your great sorrow at the loss of your gallant husband. May God in His spiritual love give you faith and strength to bear bravely your loss and loneliness."

Lieutenant Scott's brother, Sergeant Harry Scott, has nine years' service in the Dragoon Guards and has been in France for three years, while his father, Mr. Harry Scott, served in the 15th Hussars for over twenty years. Mrs. Scott, widow of the gallant young officer has five brothers serving in the Army, of whom four are now in France and the other has returned to England after having been gassed.

Mrs. Scott, widow, and Mr. and Mrs. H. Scott, father and mother of Lieutenant Scott, desire to return their sincere thanks for the many kind expressions of sympathy which have reached them in their bereavement.

11

SEARCHING THROUGH old issues of the *Camberley News* and records of the war, I could not fail to notice the number of bravery awards and I read with admiration the accounts of their deeds on the field of battle. I investigated those that I personally found the most interesting.

13 November 1915, 2nd Lt. John Bessell M.C:
He was in the 3rd Dorset Regiment attached to the Royal Fusiliers. On 27th September 1915 he made a daring reconnaissance of the north face and ascertained the position of the German bombing party. He then directed the bombing party, dislodged the Germans and occupied and held the trench under heavy bombing. He held out until he was wounded. His bravery and resource were mainly instrumental in preventing the enemy from outflanking the battalion. Before the war he had been on the staff of Barclay's Bank.

15 July 1916,
Sgt. Major Drake, DCM:
His home was at "Heloise", Moorlands Road and he started service with the Queens Royal West Surrey Regiment in the first Battalion. He served in the Indian Campaign 1897 /1898 with the clasps for Tirah and Punjab Frontier. He also served through the South African War with the Queens and took part in the Defence of Lady- smith. He was awarded Queen Victoria's Medal with 6 clasps—Belfast, Laings, Nek, Orange Free State, Defence of Lady- smith, Elandslaagte and Cape Colony. He joined the Military Mounted Police and served for 12 months in France where he won the DCM. From there he was sent to Salonica.

30th September 1916, Bomb. William Edward Beedell MM:
He served with the Royal Field Artillery and lived at Prospect Place York Town, where he attended school. After German shelling had blown up some dug outs, he volunteered to go and rescue some of the injured men, who were buried. After three attempts, the last under particu- larly heavy fire with a shell whislting past every two minutes, he rescued the last man. He received the ribbon on the field of battle and was congratulated by his colonel. He had had a narrow escape on a previous occasion when a bullet went right through his service cap.

GALLANTRY AWARDS

18th November 1916, Cpl. W. Sharpe MM:
His home was 72 Park Street and he was in the Queens Royal West Surrey Regiment attached to a trench mortar battery. He was decorated for gallantry and devotion to duty in the taking of Schwaben Ridout. He was presented with the ribbon by his general who congratulated him on winning it.

9th June 1917, Sgt. S.W. Hammond MM:
He enlisted with the Royal Berkshire Regiment in 1903 and made his home with his sister in Princess Street. He won his MM at the Battle of the Somme when he was 32 years old. On another occasion his distinguished conduct was brought to the notice of his General. He died on the front line trench and a letter was sent to his sister by his commanding officer Lt. A.W. Breach: *"Madam, I expect before now you will have heard the sad news of the death of your brother Sgt. S.W. Hammond. He was killed in the front line trench on 27th April and I can assure you that his death was instantaneous. He was a splendid soldier and was beloved by both his officers and men. He had a charming personality and did not know the meaning of the word fear. I as his Company Commander shall miss him more than I can say. Please accept my deepest sympathy."*

29th September 1917, L/Corporal D. Brown MM:
He served with the Queens Royal West Surrey Regiment. The Germans were attacking with 'flaming fire' and he worked hard with his machine gun, playing havoc among the enemy who were prevented from reaching the trench in his part of the line. He was well known in Camberley as a regular player with the Camberley and York Town Football Team, and before that had played for the old Camberley St. Georges Football Club with great success.

10th November 1917, CSM James Nunn DCM MM:
He was in the Hampshire Regiment and had won the MM in the Dardenelles. He was an old York Town schoolboy and his parents lived at "Rylestones", Moorlands Road, Camberley. He took part in the Battle of the Somme, and Ypres where he was awarded the DCM. Although shot just below one of his temples, he continued to control his Lewis Gun for another two and a half hours with valuable results to our force. A letter from his Major General states: *"CSM J Nunn of the Hampshire Regiment. I wish to place on record my appreciation of your gallantry and devotion to duty on 20th and 21st September when, with a few men, you rushed an enemy strongpoint which threatened to hold up the whole Brigade advance. After this, with a party of men, you were the first to reach your objectives although you were wounded in the advance, and when the enemy launched a counter attack and all of your officers had become casualties, you took command and sent back very valuable reports to Brigade Headquarters."*
He was born in Camberley and was killed at Flanders on 30th June 1918.

22 September 1916, Temp. 2nd Lt. Henry Cope Evans DSO:
It proved quite difficult to ascertain details of how he received his DSO and it was only after seven letters that I finally did so. He was born on 26th July 1979 and lived at "West Point", Camberley. He held a Royal Aero Club Pilot's Certificate and qualified at the Military School, Farn- borough on a Maurice Farman Biplane on 23rd March 1916.

DISTINGUISHED SERVICE ORDER
Temporary 2nd Lieutenant Henry Cope EVANS
General List attached to the Royal Flying Corps
For conspicuous gallantry and skill on many occasions in attacking hostile aircraft, frequently against large odds. In one fortnight he brought down 4 enemy machines, returning on one occasion with his machine badly damaged.

EVANS, Henry Cope ____2603
West Point, Camberley.
Born 26th July 1979 at London
Nationality British
Rank, Regiment, Profession 2nd Lieut. General List
Certificate taken on Maurice Farman Biplane
At Military School, Farnborough
Date 23rd March 1916
Killed 3rd September 1916.

CASUALTY CARD. Tests completed _____
Went overseas _____

Rank, Name and Unit Evans 2/Lt. HC - DSO
Genl List RFC 24 Syd
Graduated as 20 on (date) 19.12.15 At Time of Accident _____
Employed as _____

Date Report Received and Official Reference.	Date of Casualty	Where occurred.	Type of Machine.	Nature and Cause of Accident.	Result of Accident.	Name of other Occupant of Machine.	Remarks
5.9.16 Rec'd. 7.9.16	3.9.16	France 24 Sq	de Nav Scout	missing	Prob/w	none	German List 215 1/77
Dead Report Recvd 3.4.17				Death accepted for offl purposes			

He was serving in France with the No. 24 Squadron and went missing on 3rd September 1916 while flying a De Havilland Scout. He was taken prisoner of war but his death was reported on 13th April 1917.

The citation for his DSO was published in the *London Gazette* on 22nd September 1916 and reads *"For conspicuous gallantry and skill on many occasions in attacking hostile aircraft, frequently against large odds. In one fortnight he brought down four enemy machines, returning on one occasion with his machine badly damaged."*

The insignia and warrant were sent to his wife at Camberley on 20th August 1917, and were acknowledged the following day. According to records, he is buried in Arras Memorial at Faubourg D'Amiens Cen., Arras in France.

23rd November 1918, Ltd. Osbert W. Jackman MM:

He was the eldest of three boys and lived with his parents in Kings Ride, Camberley. At one time all three boys and their father were serving in France. He was the second of the boys to be killed. In June 1915 he enlisted in the Royal Berkshire Regiment in which he was later promoted to the rank of Sgt. Major. He went to France and took part in the Battle of the Somme and was awarded the M.M. for devotion to duty and gallantry at Zillebeke. He joined the Queens Royal West Surrey Regiment on 5th September 1918 as an officer and returned to France where he served with the 1st Battalion.

To find details of how he died I referred to the Battalion Diary which gave details on a day by day account of what action they were involved in. The battalion was under the command of Lt. Col. Hon H. Ritchie D.S.O. Scottish Rifles.

"7 Nov. 1918 Battalion moved forward in artillery formation. Took village of Ecuelyn and found line east of the village. Strong opposition was encountered on entering the village. Village was secured by 09.20. Casualties: Jackman killed, 5 other ranks killed, 6 other ranks missing."

The corporal who was with him brought his body back for burial and he is buried in Ecuelyn Churchyard, France.

The 7th November 1918 was the last day on which the 1st Battalion was in action during the war as the Armistice was signed four days later. How unlucky and sad to have been killed so close to the end of all the hostilities. Imagine how his parents must have felt.

1st June 1918, Sgt. A.W. Denyer DCM:

He served with the Queens Royal West Surrey Regiment and was an old York Town boy. His award was for conspicuous gallantry and devotion to duty. The citation for his award was: 206607 Cpl. A.W. Denyer—*London Gazette* 1 May 1918. *"For conspicuous gallantry and devotion to duty. When the officers and the company sergeant major became casualties he took command, though wounded himself, and refused to withdraw until*

another officer arrived. He repelled a counter attack with great skill, and stood up under heavy fire with utter disregard of danger in order to bomb the enemy more accurately."

19th January 1918, Flight Sgt. Enos E. White, Meritorious Service Medal:

He joined the Royal Flying Corps in June 1915. He received his medal at 22 years of age for valuable service rendered on the field. Before joining up he worked with Frederic Robinson the photographer where he served his apprenticeship. He was the first local man to win this particular award. His parents lived at Portesbury Road Camberley. I spoke to his daughter and pointed out to her that a copy of this particular paper was on display in the Museum when last it was opened and she read it with avid interest. She also showed me a copy of the extract which

was taken from the *London Gazette* 1st January 1918. *"His Majesty the King has been graciously pleased to approve of the award of Meritorious Service Medal to the undermentioned Warrant Officers and Men in recognition of valuable services rendered with the Armies in the Field during the present War."*

I don't think I can end this chapter any better than by quoting the King's words to the Field Marshall at the end of the War:

"No words can express my feelings of admiration for the glorious British Army whose splendid bravery under your leadership has now achieved this magnificent success over the enemy. You have fought without ceasing for the past four years. My warmest congratulations to you and your undaunting Army, where all ranks with mutual confidence in each other have faced hardships and dangers with dogged resolution and have fought on with an irresistible determination that has now resulted in this final and overwhelming victory."

BUCKINGHAM PALACE.

TO MY PEOPLE

At this grave moment in the struggle between my people and a highly organised enemy who has transgressed the Laws of Nations and changed the ordinance that binds civilized Europe together, I appeal to you.

I rejoice in my Empire's effort, and I feel pride in the voluntary response from my Subjects all over the world who have sacrificed home, fortune, and life itself, in order that another may not inherit the free Empire which their ancestors and mine have built.

I ask you to make good these sacrifices.

The end is not in sight. More men and yet more are wanted to keep my Armies in the Field, and through them to secure Victory and enduring Peace.

In ancient days the darkest moment has ever produced in men of our race the sternest resolve.

I ask you, men of all classes, to come forward voluntarily and take your share in the fight.

In freely responding to my appeal, you will be giving your support to our brothers, who, for long months, have nobly upheld Britain's past traditions, and the glory of her Arms.

George R.I.

THIS WAS the main regiment which local Camberley men joined in the Great War and for this reason I have included a short history of it, as well as some other facts and information:

1661/84:	Raised as The Tangier Regiment of Foot
1684/86:	Regiment styled The Queen's Regiment
1703:	Made a Royal Regiment
1715/27:	Her RH The Princess of Wales Own Regiment of Foot
1727-51:	The Queen's Own Royal Regiment of Foot
1751/1881:	The 2nd or Queen's Royal Regiment of Foot
1881/1921:	The Queen's Royal West Surrey Regiment
1921/1959:	The Queen's Royal Regiment (West Surrey)
1959:	Amalgamated with East Surrey Regiment to form the Queen's Royal Surrey Regiment
1969:	1st Battalion The Queen's Regiment and the County affiliation ceased.

The motto of the Royal West Surrey was "Vex Exuviæ Triumphant" which means "Even in defeat there can be triumph."

The motto today is "Pristinæ Virtutis Memore" which means "Mindful of the Gallant Actions of the Past", which I think is very appropriate.

In the First World War they saw service at many places:

1914, 1917, 1918: Retreat from Mons, Ypres
1916, 1918: Somme
1917: Messino
1915: Gallipoli
1917, 1918: Gallipoli
1915, 1918: Mesopotania
1916, 1917: North West Frontier

At the start of the war, the Regiment landed at Le Havre and a message from the King was read out to them:

"You are leaving home to fight for the safety and honour of my empire. Belgium, whose country we are pledged to defend, has been attacked, and France is about to be invaded by the same powerful foe.
I have implicit confidence in you, my soldiers. Duty is your watchword, and I know your duty will be nobly done.
I shall follow your every movement with deepest interest and mark with eager satisfaction your daily progress, indeed your welfare will never be absent from my thoughts.
I pray God to bless you and guard you and bring you back victorious."

At this time they were eight miles from Le Havre.

Apart from the Royal West Surrey, the other local regiments were the East Surrey, The Royal West Kent, The Royal Berks and the Hampshire Regiment. Following is a table of decorations received during the war.

The uniform and equipment (front and back views) worn in France and Flanders during the Great War.

ROYAL WEST SURREY REGIMENT

	Other Decorations	VCs	Killed
East Surrey	62	7	6750
Royal West Surrey	74	4	8000
Royal West Kent	69	3	6900
East Kent	48	1	6000
Royal Berkshire Regiment	55	2	7140
Hampshire Regiment	82	3	7580

When one looks at those figures of the two Surrey Regiments it is nearly 15,000 young men, mostly local, who were killed. It must have been absolutely awful for their families waiting at home, dreading the letter from France or elsewhere telling them of the loss of a husband, father, son or brother.

In the *Camberley News* of April 1917 a list of German casualties for the month of March, and of total casualties were given. Dreadful loss of life not only for them, but for all countries involved in the war.

	March 1917	Total
Killed and died of wounds	10,863	962,760
Died of sickness	2,679	63,920
Prisoners	1,158	281,943
Missing	5,089	250,915
Severely wounded	8,154	552,911
Wounded	3,896	304,807
Slightly wounded	18,248	1,550,786
Wounded and remaining with their units	4,716	234,924

FRITH HILL CAMP was on the common land opposite Brompton Hospital near, surprisingly enough, Frith Hill. It was used for many German prisoners of war, as well as for internees, and held quite a few thousand inmates.

By September 1914 there was talk of extending the Camp (which at this time contained no less than 1300 German Prisoners of War) to increase the capacity to over 10,000.

A report of 26th September states that 1600 Germans captured at the Battles of the Marne and Aisne had arrived at Frith Hill. They were transported to Frimley in two special trains and with only one exception, all marched to the camp. The exception was one who had a leg injury and he was taken up by the regimental transport which had come for their luggage. The prisoners were all surprised at the attitude of the local people who gave them gifts of tobacco, cigarettes, cakes, fruit and ginger beer. One of the prisoners said that he knew some good old English swear words, and when the Kaiser's name was mentioned the report states he said "D--- the Kaiser!" (Strong words indeed).

By October both military and naval prisoners were arriving and the number of visitors was increasing. One of the officers who was regulating traffic described it as worse than that experienced at Ascot Races.

A local businessman who had to go to the camp on business, parked his motor cycle in the compound, only to have one of the prisoners remark, "I see you cannot make do without some things made in Germany." He had noticed the Bosch Magneto on the machine. The *Camberley News* did not lose the opportunity to use this story and went on to say that the German, who spoke good English, when not involved in the art of assisting to spread Prussian *kultur*, mutilating the wounded, killing defenceless women and children, and destroying cathedrals and homes; was engaged in a motor business in Germany. *Kultur* is described as the German conception of the benefits of civilisation to be imposed on all others.

At the end of October, a further train full of 200 more prisoners arrived and this attracted many Farnborough people to the station. Many of them were only about 16 years old and seemed very happy to be away from the horrors of war; they had come from Flanders.

Around this time, there was an article in the *Camberley News* concerning the arrival of the German prisoners. Under a sub-heading of "NO NEED TO FEAR THE GERMANS", they were described as being "... *all sorts and stamps. The average physique was not as good as the average of a battalion of a British Infantry on service at the present time, and far below that of the battalions of Kitchener's Army that had embarked for France during 1915. Some of the men were puny in physique, but the general impression was of fat, round faces, small eyes close together and bullet heads. I thought if this is a fair specimen*

German prisoners of war at Frith Hill, Frimley
photo courtesey of Surrey Heath Museum

FRITH HILL CONCENTRATION CAMP

of the Germany Army of today, our men need never fear any Germans who come over the Rhine.

As I watched the column swing by, my mind reverted to the stories told by wounded British soldiers who had fallen into the Germans' hands, and contrasted the treatment meted out to them with what was accorded to the German prisoners as they passed the silent spectators in that village street. I thought of the brutal ill-treatment by the German guards on the train. Wretched British prisoners crowded into the cattle trucks, starving and begging for water; of the stones and filth flung at them and of the misery of long journeys by rail and road in the depths of winter without overcoats, and in many cases without boots.

I thought of the horrors of Wittenberg camp, and then I thanked God that I had seen the British reception of German prisoners and the lessons it contained, and hoped that among the prisoners in that column were some with first hand knowledge of the savage way in which British prisoners had been treated under similar circumstances, so that they could compare it with the experience of that day."

Patriotic stuff! Another thing is that in those days very few people went abroad so this was the first time many people had seen any Germans at all, let alone "the enemy".

The *Camberley News* of 28th November 1914 announced that the whole of the Austrian and German civilian aliens who had been interned at Frith Hill had been removed to the Isle of Man. This did not affect the Army or Naval personnel whose numbers were swelled by the addition of one infantry officer, one naval officer and 16 sailors received from Chatham. They all belonged to the German Cruiser *"Mainz"*, which had been sunk at the end of August in Heligoland.

On 27th March 1915 the camp re-opened after having been closed for alterations; the prisoners had been removed to the Isle of Man or onto ships at Portsmouth and

German prisoners marching from Frimley Station

Frith Hill Camp and Prisoners of War Compound

Southend during the closure. It would now be used exclusively for Army and Naval personnel—no civilians at all—and those prisoners in it before its closure would not return.

By May of that year there were over 2,000 prisoners and the arrival of a special steam train brought in another 400 who all marched along singing *"Tipperary".* At the junction of the Frimley and Portsmouth Roads the signpost to London seemed to provide a great source of amusement.

In October of the same year the description in the press of the latest arrivals must have done wonders for the propaganda machine: it said that while most of them were dressed in the German uniform, some wore corduroy trousers and sea boots, and could be without doubt, described as the roughest lot to have been brought in. The "Hun" were bedraggled and unkempt.

GERMAN PRISONERS ESCAPE FROM FRITH HILL

This was the headline of the *Camberley News* on 30th September 1916. It transpired that after their return from work, five were found to be missing—four sailors and an aircraftsman. A hue and cry was at once raised and the names of the escapees were sent through to the Police Stations at Camberley and Aldershot as well as to Scotland Yard. Special Constables were called out. Sgt. Kenward from Camberley attended with three bloodhounds and tracked them as far as Brookwood. Nothing was seen of them however, until the next day when three of them were caught near Ascot by a Special Constable who found them asleep by the roadside, and took them to a nearby hotel, where they were escorted back by a detachment of the Royal Flying Corps. They said they had kept to the woods and only travelled by night, and they were glad to surrender. (Bound to say that, of course).

With the announcement of the signing of the armistice in November 1918 and the ending of hostilities, the prisoners' mood changed. They made no secret of their pleasure and when they marched to the railway station on their way back to the camp it was generally commented that they looked far happier than usual and many were laughing or smiling and noticing the flags and bunting in Camberley with considerable interest. One prisoner remarked that he was glad and that he would soon be home with his mother for Christmas. The *Camberley News* commented: "Apparently he looks on the Armistice as a quick means of returning to the Fatherland."

I should think life in the camp and working in the Camberley area was most acceptable. Far better than trench warfare in France or wherever. It was a familiar sight to see troops of prisoners marching down to the train and many were given small gifts of chocolate or cigarettes, mostly by people who had sons in the war in France, and hoped that their sons would be treated in the same way.

photos courtesey of Surrey Heath Museum

A book written about the history of Brompton Hospital refers only once to the camp. In October 1914 a letter was sent to the War Office complaining that—in a quaintly worded phrase—"the contents of sanitary arrangements from the Concentration Camp nearby were being deposited close to the Sanatorium and causing offence." What a nice way to express it. There is no note of any reply.

During the war at least three German prisoners died at the camp in 1914 and were all buried in Deepcut Military Cemetery. I visited the cemetery to find out their details, but was told that they had all three been exhumed in 1962 and it was not known where they were now. A letter to Germany addressed to the Volksbund Deutsch Kriegsgraberfursorge soon brought the information I was looking for. This is the German War Graves Commission which is like our Commonwealth War Graves Commission in Maidenhead.

On 4th September 1914, Obermaschinenmaat Robert Adler, born 11 November 1884 was buried, having died of pneumonia. He was a sailor from the *"Konigin Luise".* *

On 16th October Landwehrmann Josef Gilles, 36 years, died. He was buried on 19th October. His death is recorded as accidental and no other details are given. (I wonder what that was all about). He was in the 11/53 Reserve Infantry Regiment.

On 12th November Gemeiner Wilhelm Schneips, 23 years, died from septic poisoning. He was buried on 16th November. He was in the same regiment as Josef Gilles.

All three were exhumed on 25th October 1962 and are now buried together, side by side in the German Military Cemetery at Cannock Chase, north of Birmingham.

This ship appeared in the 1951 film 'African Queen' starring Humphrey Bogart.

photos courtesey of Surrey Heath Museum

German Prisoners at Frimley en route for Frith Hill.

German prisoners at Frimley Railway Station

German War Cemetery at Cannock Chase, Staffs

Prisoners (including some from the *Mainz*)

The Crusier *Mainz*, one of the German warships sunk in the Bight of Heliogland on Aug. 24 1914.

PLOUGHING THROUGH the back copies of the *Camberley News*, I could not fail to be amused by the reports pertaining to cases at the Court, not only the actual cases themselves, but the remarks and sentences passed. How times change. Court today, and I speak from personal experience, bears little resemblance to the cases mentioned here or in my previous book. It was a different world then. Better or worse? One could argue for many hours about that I think.

In January 1914 Mr. Chasmore Gates was up before the Court for driving at a speed in excess of 20mph in the London Road. Two Police Officers gave evidence that they saw him driving at between 35 and 40 mph and when PC Stevens signalled him to stop, shouting at him at the same time, he failed to do so. The defendent stated that he did not hear the officer shout at him. He was fined 40/- for speeding and let off failing to stop. In addition he had to pay 2/6d. costs.

Two weeks later Col. H.S. Jeudewine pleaded guilty to riding a bicycle on the footpath in Portsmouth Road. He said, *"I went onto the footpath as there were large stones in the road, the road was quite impassable at this spot. It was usually thought that when a road was being repaired, for one half to be done at a time so allowing the other half to remain open to traffic. In this case the stones were over all the road and not rolled in."* The Chairman agreed with him but justice had to be administered and he was fined 7/6d.

On 14th February there were various cases at Court including a man fined 7/6d. for cruelly kicking a dog. Frederick Courtenege was fined 5/- for not having his name printed on his van, and a further 5/- for not having his van constructed so as to give him a clear view of the highway. There were similar fines for people riding bicycles on footpaths. (I wonder why the Colonel was fined 7/6d. the previous month).

On 28th February 1914, A.E. Wise and F.E. Parker were both fined 5/- as householders whose chimneys accidentally caught fire. (Can you imagine that happening today?) On 14th March, Frederick Hulbert was summoned for not having his name and address on his cart. He pleaded guilty, but gave a very plausible excuse to the Court. *"It arose through an act of kindness on my part. I lent the cart to someone whose cart had broken down. I have lived among you gentlemen for 23 years and have come from Lightwater with my cart loaded with vegetables and sometimes with fat pigs* (laughter) *and I have never been summoned before. I was the good samaritan and for being a good samaritan I am summoned here. I am always good and a good law abider.* (laughter) *I ask you to dismiss the summons because I was helping someone out of a hole. I don't see how it is an offence."* After some further questions the Chairman Mr. Temple Cooke let him off under the First Offenders Act. Again, there was much laughter in Court.

COURT CASES

J. Temple Cooke, JP

On 23rd May there was a prosecution by the NSPCC Inspector Dunn. Robert 11 and Rose 8 were found in a verminous state, ragged clothes and black all over. There was no woman in the house and the father and the children slept in one bed, the bedding of which was dirty. They lived in Belmont Road. Their father Issac was sent to prison for one month with hard labour. The surname of the family was Clarke (no relation though).

In October 1914 two 12-year old lads were up before the children's court for throwing stones in the highway. As usual at this time of the year the lads were throwing at horse chestnut trees. They were let off with a caution and were

told to tell their comrades that the next lad prosecuted for throwing stones would not be let off so lightly. How would they have dealt with the children of today who appear before the Juvenile Court? The mind boggles.

"A man who was drunk in Park Street in November kept asking the Constable to lock him up," so said Sgt. Kenward in evidence. *"When he extended the same request to me, I duly obliged him."* For his trouble Harry Langham was fined 5/-. He might as well have ridden his bicycle on the footpath and got his moneysworth!

1915 saw a different case at Court, one related to the War. Arthur Giles was summoned by Major Lamb of the Rifle Brigade for impeding the movement of troops. The troops were marching along when they met the defendent with a coal cart. He was asked to allow the troops to pass but refused. A Sgt. went to hold the horse but was struck by the defendent. He also tried to drive towards the troops but they managed to get past. He pleaded 'not guilty' but was found guilty and fined 5/-. This was the first case of this kind to be heard at the Court.

In April of the same year a soldier was fined 4/- for driving a car without having a driving licence. He thought that as he was in the Army he could drive any vehicle without a licence.

On 3rd July 1915 under the heading of "A WARNING TO LADS" the *Camberley News* reported that three young lads, Leonard and Eric Chambers and Stanley Morton were all summoned for damaging growing grass by the Blackwater River in June. P.C. Reid gave evidence that the lads, after bathing in the river, (I would not recommend that now) and not having towels, had rolled around in the grass to get dry, and the last two named had run about in two fields all laid up for hay. They had caused a great deal of damage and were an intolerable nuisance. The Chairman, Mr. Temple Cooke, hoped that this case might act as a deterrent to the boys and to others in the neighbourhood but let the boys off lightly with fines of 2/6d. each. Other boys similarly summoned would be more severely dealt with.

In January 1916 things were getting bad; two lads were fined 2/6d. for firing catapults in Yorktown and two other lads were fined 2/- for riding bicycles on the footpath.

On 25th March, Albert Nunn who had been stopped at 9.30pm the week before by PC Page at Frimely Green for not having a red rear lamp, was fined 5/-. Unfortunately for him, at 10.15pm the same night he was stopped by PC Holland for the same reason. The second offence cost him 7/6d. I expect that taught him! After the second offence it was stated he got back on his cycle and rode off.

On 20th May, Sgt. Kenward and his fellow officers must have had a busy day in the Frimley Road for it was stated in Court that they had timed 23 Aldershot & District buses and only two of them had exceeded the 12mph speed limit. It was over a badly repaired part of the road which had been the subject of many complaints. Both drivers were fined 10/-, and the bench hoped it would not escape the notice of other drivers in the area and so act as a warning.

In June there was a case at Court which was somewhat different from the usual type of case. Camille Danneau, a Belgian ex-soldier was charged with coming to live in a prohibited area and entering a prohibited area without an identity book. He created a scene in Court by crying violently, and this was renewed when Sgt. Kenward started to give his evidence. He had been drinking in a bar of a local public house with a married woman resident. The defendent was married and had two children. When asked what he was doing he stated he had come from Staines for a fortnight. He had also called at the Police Station. He admitted not having an identity book but said the police in Staines had said he could come. He was given two hours to "clear out" from the district and was seen getting on a train. He had obviously returned and had been seen about town, arm in arm with a married woman in public houses. This had caused a great deal of unpleasantness between the woman and her husband. The Court decided that he had not taken the opportunity to leave when it was given to him and that there was no excuse. He would have to pay a fine of £10 or go to prison for one month in default.

On 13th January 1917, a man who was driving down the London Road towards Camberley was summoned for driving at a speed in excess of the 20mph speed limit. PC Pink had signalled him to stop but on seeing that he was not able to do so, jumped out of the way. The car stopped some 47 yards down the road. The two officers estimated the speed to be fully 35 mph. The defendent, a James Peter Wright, asked in Court if the officer had any right to stop him if both officers did not have stop watches. He was told they did, to which he replied *"Then your Honour, I am guilty."* As he was a chauffeur he was only fined £1 instead of the usual £2. (Lucky man?).

In February Mr. C.V. Wright was in Court for riding a cycle without lights. When stopped by a police officer he said, *"I have just returned from Africa and we are allowed to ride without lights there."* Didn't make any difference though—fined 10/-.

Although the following case was heard at Aldershot I have included it because I am sure that like me, you will find it interesting. On 22nd September 1917, Thomas Stevens, a man of middle age, was summoned by Edith Nash for common assault. Miss Nash, aged 21, was sitting in the compartment of a train when Mr. Stevens entered and said *"When are you going to meet me?"* to which she replied *"Never"*. He asked her why not and gave her three plums which she placed on the seat.

He then sat beside her, placed his arms around her and started to kiss her (how bold). She struggled away from him

Alderman A.C. Pain, C.C., J.P.
(Camberley Magistrate during war period, later chairman 1925-27)

and pulled the communication cord. At Aldershot, when Inspector Wright left for a moment, the defendent had offered Miss Nash £5 "to let the matter drop." She had replied, *"No, I want to put a stop to it."* When spoken to by Police, he said *"I didn't think she minded so I don't see any harm in it."* He admitted committing an act of indiscretion and asked the Bench to overlook it and assured them it would not happen again. He did not think Miss Nash resented it, otherwise he would not have done it. The Chairman said the defendant's action was uncalled for. *"In these times when many women had to travel about unprotected it behoved them to deal with such cases with a certain amount of severity. The defendant had a good character and he hoped this was but an isolated case of indiscretion and in these circumstances the magistrates must fine him £2. 2s. or one month in prison in default."*

On 23rd March 1918 George Henry Batt, a ganger of Blackdown Camp, pleaded guilty but ignorant of the charge of receiving a military overcoat at Deepcut. He had been stopped by two Military Policemen in Minden Road with the overcoat in a brown paper parcel. When asked

what it was he had told them it was 'washing'. Upon opening the parcel and disclosing its contents, he said he had bought the coat for 2/- from a soldier who had said he wanted a drink. When charged by good old Sgt. Kenward under the Army Act he said, *"The soldier wanted a drink of beer and I gave him 2/- for it but I didn't know it was an overcoat. I am as innocent as a donkey, sir."* (laughter). His explanation was not accepted and he was fined 40/- plus 23/- (the value of the overcoat) and in addition 6/- for the hire of the taxicab in which he was taken to the Police Station. (Justice with a difference?).

I will end with a case that took place on 29th June 1918 when Leonard Ayres, Ronald Mullins, Leonard Mullins, Sidney Harker, Cecil Bellingham, Frederick Downer, Leonard Dobson, John Hutton and Bertie Parker were all charged with stealing a quantity of fruit valued at 5/- from Sherborne House, the property of Sir Arthur Hammond V.C. K.C.B., D.S.O. The boys all pleaded guilty. This sort of thing had happened to Sir Arthur before and he was determined to prosecute although the value of the fruit was only 5/-. Over a period of time 21 gooseberry bushes had been stripped. They were all bound over in the sum of £1 to be of good behaviour for the next six months with their parents as joint securities. In addition, each had to pay 2/6d. costs. The Bench hoped this would act as a warning as there was a great deal of this sort of stealing going on in the district. I spoke to Ron Mullins recently and he remembered it well, although he was only 8 years old at the time.

The Courthouse was originally built in 1905. This photograph was taken quite recently, before it was modernised.

19

SINCE ITS FIRST edition on the 11th March 1905, the *Camberley News* has been the main focal point for the residents of the area to read about what is going on in the Town. It also gave them an opportunity through the "Letters to the Editor" page to have their points of view printed.

In that first edition there were adverts for coke—16s 8d a ton! Also the appointment of a Headmistress at the Yorktown Schools at a salary of £65 a year. An advert for a dentist showed one set of teeth for 1 guinea or 2s 6d for a single tooth. This was in the time of peace before the First World War changed the lives of everyone in the Town.

What one has to remember is that there was no radio or television and the only method of finding out about life on the front, as well as other news, was to read the *Camberley News*, still priced at 1d, the same as it was in 1905. By reading it each week one was able to find out the unfortunate families who had lost relatives at the front, and also to see what they could do to support the war effort by making articles for the soldiers or by donating items for the three homes for wounded soldiers that were situated in the Town.

During the war period the paper consisted of just a double sheet but how important it was, not only for the people left at home, but also for the soldiers mostly in France who could keep in touch with what was going on during their absence.

What I did find sad was that there was hardly a week without the loss of some local man, reported in a column called the "Roll of Honour". I have included the names of some of these in a separate chapter. There was another column which gave details of the many awards for bravery won by local men, again I have included some of those in a separate chapter.

During those dark days of the War all, or most of the news in the paper was concerned with the War, although there were little bits of news about the Rabbit Club or what was going on at Court in that particular week.

The ADVENTURES of BILL THE BOS'UN

Written and Illustrated by Wm. McMANN.

RATION BOOKS.

"Ration Books 'as done the trick, sir."
It was Bill the Bo'sun spoke.
"They ensure fair distribution
Of the grub among us folk.
Everyone now gets 'is rations,
Working man an' millionaire,
An' there ain't no fear o' gluttons
Gettin' half a dozen's share.

"Everybody gets their share."

"Tho' it's 'ard, sir, to believe it,
There are gluttons 'ereabout;
Food 'ogg's wot the papers call 'em,
Who would never go without,
Tho' the rest of us was starvin'.
Lost to shame, they'd eat their fill,
Without thought of friend or neighbour,
Food 'oggs, that's the name," said Bill.

Then old Bill grew reminiscent:
"Food 'oggs, sir, ain't nothin' new;
Every bloomin' country has 'em,
Right, sir, an' I've met 'em, too.
Still, ye'd 'ardly think ye'd meet 'em
Where the stately palm trees grow,
In the South Pacific Islands;
But I did, sir—years ago.

"I'm a Food 'Ogg!"

"Food 'oggs in the South Pacific
Differ from the breed we've got:
They don't see no sense in hoarding;
No, they eat it on the spot—
Eat it till there ain't no wrinkles,
Eat until their skin's so tight
That they cannot close their eyelids!
Food 'oggs! That's the word all right.

"But I'd better tell the story.
It was touch an' go with me,
An' occurred w'en I was tradin'
In the South Pacific Sea.
Wrecked upon a coral reef, sir;
Bottom out the ship was tore,
An' of all the crew aboard 'er,
I alone was cast ashore.

Senseless first, I woke a captive;
'Ands were bound with ropes o' grass,
An' a savage chief demanded,
With a frown, my landing pass!
'Who are you?' I arsks the fellow,
For I didn't like 'is looks,
'I'm a Food 'Ogg,' an' he chuckled,
''An' my hobby's Ration Books'!

"Now the seasoning," says he.

"'Course, I'd no sich thing, an told 'im.
'All the worse for you,' 'e said.
'If I cannot draw yer rations,
You will 'ave to do instead!'
'Wot d'ye mean?' 'Is club he lifted;
'In this country might is right.
You're a tasty-looking morsel,
And—I've got an appetite!'

"There was I, sir, bound an' 'elpless,
Lookin' round, I quickly saw
They were cannibals, an' wondered
Whether he would eat me raw,
Or if he'd prefer to stew me—
Serve me up all pipin' 'ot!
Then I sees it was the latter,
For the chap got out the pot!

A cruiser sent a shell!

"In a trice 'e 'ad me in it,
An' it 'eld me easily;
Filled it 'arf-way up with water.
'Now the seasonin',' says he—
Carrots, turnips, salt and pepper
He'd soon added to the pot,
An' before 'e put the lid on,
Added some nice young shalot!

"I 'ad just begun to simmer,
W'en a cruiser sent a shell.
Bang!—it blew the chap to atoms;
Nearly did me in as well!
An' I never read o' food 'oggs
But," said Bill. "I seems to see
That one in the South Pacific,
Who near made a meal o' me!"

Camberley News

These were regular articles in the *Pictorial Supplement* of the Camberley News which appeared in 1918.

By this stage of the war, rationing had become more stringent as these articles and advertisements reflect. Great emphasis was put upon utilising spare ground for allotments, and the public were implored to economise in all directions to help with the war effort, even to saving their fruit stones which were used in the making of explosives.

KITCHEN RECIPES IN WAR-TIME.

Baked Herrings. — INGREDIENTS. — 2 fresh herrings, 1 onion, vinegar, water, spice, salt.

METHOD.—Split the herrings in half and remove the back-bone, roll up each half and place in a pie-dish. Cover with vinegar diluted with a little water, add the onion finely sliced, salt, some peppercorns, a clove, and a few whole spice. Cover the dish and bake in the oven until tender. Place the rolls of fish, when cold, in a glass dish, cover with the liquid strained, and serve.

Economical Cherry Tart.—INGREDIENTS.— $\frac{1}{2}$ lb. cherries, $\frac{1}{4}$ lb. short pastry, cupful boiled rice, 2 ozs. sugar.

METHOD. — Stew cherries with sugar in a little water and allow to cool. Roll out pastry and line small patty pans, bake and allow to get cold. Half-fill with rice, pour a little juice and half a dozen cherries on the top of each. Remember to save the stones for te Ministry of Munitions.

MC.

WAR-TIME GARDEN WORK & ALLOTMENT INTERESTS.

It is not generally known that broad beans may be made to produce another crop of pods after the first lot have been gathered. The plants should be cut back to 6in. from the ground, the soil around the plants well hoed, and a little liquid manure given. In a short time new shoots will appear, and these may generally be relied upon to produce a second crop of beans during the autumn before the frosts come.

* * * *

Celery plants planted out early will now be large enough for blanching. The method of using stiff bands of brown paper is one which is becoming increasingly popular. But this year, with paper not so cheap as it used to be, the more old-fashioned method of mounding will be found preferable, provided the work is done carefully. In any case, the roots must be well moistened before the work of blanching commences. The plants will now need attention in this matter about every ten days.

Camberley News

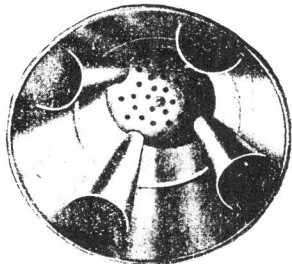

Camberley News

Despite the austerities of the War, for the lady of means there was always life's little luxuries...the most up-to-date household appliances, or the latest fashions...

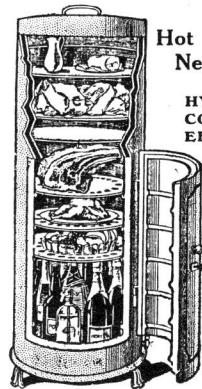

23

WAR CONDITIONS AND WOMAN'S OUTLOOK.

Before the War people used to talk a good deal about "woman's sphere." No one knew exactly what the sphere included, though it always included cooking and washing up. It was equally hard to say what was outside the sphere, but that outside were many things that were not pleasant and profitable and apparently not very difficult to do. However, talk about "the sphere" seems to be discontinued for the period of the war, which is a pity, because one of the discoveries of this troubled time is that "the sphere" provided most excellent training for the world outside it. Girls who have done housework take to engineering as a duck takes to water, and the Ministry of Munitions finds that domestic servants are amongst its best pupils in learning to make aeroplanes, shells and fuses. Housework, in fact, seems to be an education in itself.

A wise man has said that it is a good thing to know something of everything and everything about something. Now, the woman who runs a house, her own or somebody else's, has to know a little about most things. She must cook and sew, and wash, and care for children and invalids, and keep accounts, and be able to give anyone in the house a little help with his or her special business. If she can see after a garden and poultry and do household repairs so much the better, but she must still put herself down in the census paper as having "no occupation." She will very likely think that her education has been neglected, and will agree, in her heart, with those who say that she is a Jack-of-all-trades only because she can do nothing really well. She need not be despondent, for a "general" servant has a "general education" in many handicrafts, and learns a trade while a bookish woman is looking at it.

Working a bolt-tapping machine.

Camberley News

The First World War brought about drastic changes in the lives of many women...

The most pessimistic people complain that after the war no one will do housework because women will all crowd into factories. The really sensible course would be to crowd into housework in the first place as a preliminary training for the factory. To take things in this order seems to produce a woman who is good at both jobs, but the girl who begins in the factory and takes to housework on her marriage, does not so often make a success of things.

WOMEN'S WORK IN WAR TIME.

Meeting at Camberley

There was a very representative gathering of the women of the district at the Central Hall, Camberley, on Wednesday evening, when a meeting arranged conjointly by the local branches of the National Union of Women's Suffrage Societies and the National League for Opposing Women's Suffrage was held to consider "the need of our country for the help of women during the coming months and the Government scheme for the registration of women to facilitate such help." Mrs. Verran presided and was accompanied on the platform by Mrs. Basset, Mrs. Johnstone, Mrs. Rackham and Miss Margaret Douglas. The hall was crowded, many having to stand.

Opening the proceedings Mrs. Verran said the present position of affairs afforded women an opportunity for strenuous and useful work. Naturally they could not all go out as nurses but there were many works which women could and should do for the advantage of their country.

Mrs. Rackham, who dealt with the appeal of the Government to women to come forward and undertake work which would release men for service in the Army. The scheme of registering women for the work was being worked through the Labour Exchanges and up to the previous day over 50,000 women had registered. Out of the 50,000 so far only about 400 had been given work; that might seen a very small result, but the main object was to get women to register so that the Government might know what strength they had to draw upon in view of the fact that the armament firms would require the services during the next few months of a much greater number of women.

extract from *Camberley News*, Saturday May 8th, 1915

The war has thrown a searchlight upon housework in another direction. Almost every soldier has had an opportunity by now of learning how very uncomfortable a man can be who cannot cook or sew or sweep a room, and most soldiers, not liking to be more uncomfortable than necessary, have learned a little of a general servant's work. If one comes to think about it, it is unreasonable for anyone, man or woman, to be ignorant of simple household tasks as to be unable to dress himself. Even the learned men should know how to do a little of the common drudgery of the world; not to know how is to miss part of his education.

The world after the war will be full of domestic women who can make munitions, and business and professional men who have learned how to cook and sew in the army, and when they go back to their own jobs they will all be the better for their varied experience. We shall have a better understanding of the "sphere" we lived in "for the duration," whether we are cooks who have once used machine tools, or skilled mechanics who have cooked in the trenches. Before the war it sometimes seemed that people were prouder of not being able to do things than of any successful achievement. We got an absurd satisfaction out of saying that such and such things were "not our job," just as the old-fashioned people found a dignity in refusing to "demean" themselves. By the time peace comes most of us will be Jack-of-all-trades, and be proud of it.

Camberley News Pictorial Supplement
week ending August 24, 1918

E. M. G.

Working a machine that rifles naval guns.

AS IN MY PREVIOUS book, I have looked at the old school log books and I'm again including entries from the headmasters' records as they reflect the impact of the Great War upon the staff and the teaching. It is obvious from reading the school records for that time that the standards in education and discipline were affected by the loss of male teachers leaving to join the Army. It is also interesting to note that childhood illnesses which today are practically under control, in those days caused schools to be closed down for quite long periods.

YORKTOWN COUNTY PRIMARY SCHOOL

School report for 1913 states *"Class 2 & 5 are good generally; 1 and 4 are fair, the former weak in grammar, arithmetic and very weak in geography. The latter class especially weak in drawing and other manual work. The class is not strong on any subject."*

9 Feb 1914: *The floors have been washed during the weekend. Gardening Class started work today. As it is proposed to have a set of gardens in the the ground recently acquired at the back of the school, the former 14 half rod plots are being converted into one cottage garden for the senior class.*

31 March 1914: *Received a note early this afternoon from Mr. Large, woodwork instructor, that he was sending Reginald Pearce back to school owing to 'impudent and mutinous conduct' and that he had cancelled his attendance. I visited the centre and told Mr. Large that I should insist upon his correcting the alteration by recording the boy's attendance as it was not in the power of any teacher—Head or Assistant—to turn a pupil out of class and cancel his attendance owing to matters of discipline. The boy had reached the centre before my arrival. Mr. Roger, the boy's last class teacher informed me that the boy is inclined to be a bit foolish but that he had never found him impudent nor mutinous.*

There were five clases and the staff were Mr. Rogers, Mr. Smith, Mr. Harding, Mrs. Ashton and the Headmaster Mr. Ashton.

18 May 1914: *Mr. Harding has been granted leave of absence by the managers to attend the annual camp and training of the Hampshire Yeomanry to which he belongs.*

22 May 1914: *Empire Day address by Head Teacher 9.10-9.40. The timetable was suspended from 11.15 to allow the saluting of the Flag in the playground. Mr. Middleton and Messrs. Martin and Tucker were present.*

1 July 1914: *Physical Education was not taken this morning. Temperature in shade at 11 am was 80 and by 3.30 was 85.*

24 Aug 1914: *Owing to the European war at present raging, Mr. Harding has been called up with the Yeomanry and no teacher has been appointed in his place. Timetable and curriculum will have to be modified.*

Camberley School, shortly before it was demolished in 1969. Sainsbury's now stands approximately on the same site.

SCHOOLS

1 Oct 1914: *Cancelled Roy Pearson's attendance this afternoon. The father took the boy off at playtime to mind his horse, in a baker's cart. No permission was asked. The boy returned at 3.45 pm but I sent him home and notified the Managers of the matter.*

31 March 1915: *Numbers in class—Class 1, 55; Class 2, 57; Class 3, 47; Class 4, 58; Class 5, 59.*

1 June 1915: *Mr. Smith has gone today to enlist in HM Forces. Time table reorganised and altered re shortage of staff.*

27 September 1915: *A boy (G. Turner) exluded last week by school nurse for being verminous was waiting in the school yard for inspection. As he was passed satisfactory at 9.45 by the nurse, correction was made in registers by Head Teacher.* **Afternoon:** *Visit by Lord Sanger's circus—26 absentees from school. (not surprising is it?)*

9 Nov. 1915: *Owing to the fact that the streets have to be kept dark at night—no street lamp to be lighted and shop and other window lights screened—afternoon school from today will commence at 1.30 and close at 4 by instructions from Managers). Timetable to be altered accordingly.*

30 Nov. 1915: *Head Teacher absent today by permission to attend marriage of nephew home on leave from 'the front'.*

By April 1916 the classes were now smaller but with only four staff, the teachers still had large numbers of children to contend with. The following month, after 20 years' service,

Mrs. Ashton terminated her service. By October, all the male staff, with the exception of the Head Teacher had left for military service and apart from Mr. Ashton there was Miss Close and Miss Martin who each had in the region of more than 50 children to teach. The log book states *"considering the disruptions, satisfactory progress has been made."*

At the start of 1917 there were falls of snow and attendance was described as very poor, dropping from 91% to 82%. One week in February for five days the temperature was 20°, 25°, 17°, 17° and 25°.

In July the school log records *"Difficulty re teachers. Classes left to themselves. The teachers have all worked well during the term."*

26 Sept. 1917: *Jack Waite was told by his teacher to remain till 12.30. He told her that she had no right to detain him and refused to stay. On arrival this afternoon he was told to report himself to me, but instead of doing so went at once off the premises. When I called to him from the front door to come back he did not do so. Unfortunately, the conversation was not recorded, but the records show that the following day, John Waite was brought back into the school by his father and made to apologise for his conduct the previous day, in front of the class.*

14 Jan. 1918: *Miss Cancellor, Matron of Frimley Cottage Hospital visited and examined children, excluded 3 boys for impetigo.* (What's that? I hear you say. Well, it's a contagious skin disease).

11 June 1918: *The message of their Majesties the King and Queen showing their appreciation of the 'self-denial and devotion of the teachers and the keeness and patriotism of*

S.C.C. MINUTE BOOK 1918

At the request of the Board of Education, special arrangements were made throughout the County for the picking of blackberries by school children in view of the shortage of fruit for jam making. In the larger schools the attendance of children over 11 years of age engaged in picking was recognised as attendance at school, and in the smaller schools holidays were given for the purpose.

The fruit picked was collected by the Surrey and North Hants Fruit and Vegetable Association under an arrangement made by the Ministry of Food, and payment was made at the rate of 3d per lb. Returns as to the quantity of blackberries collected are not yet to hand, but it is known that in one school in each of the first two weeks of the season a ton was collected.

the youth of the country' during the present war was read to the school this morning.

On September 9th and 11th, the school closed for blackberrying.

By the end of 1918 there were 211 children at the school.

YORKTOWN PRIMARY GIRLS SCHOOL

There were at this time, (1914) three teachers, Marion Inwood, Dorothy Tegg and Ena Biles.

13 Feb 1914: *The attendance has been very low this week, so many children have colds. Average for week 128.*

9 July 1914: *Gladys and Dorothy Field excluded until it is known what their sister is suffering with.* (Wonder what it was? it doesn't say).

26 Aug 1914: *The Headmistresss resumed duties today. Owing to the outbreak of war it has been impossible for her to return from Switzerland before.*

22 Dec 1914: *The timetable will not be followed on the last lesson to allow of a little breaking up concert.*

14 July 1915: *Half day holiday granted this afternoon for the Congregational Sunday School Treat.*

19 Jan 1917: *Miss Parsons has been granted 3 days leave on the occasion of her marriage. Became Mrs. Chard.*

In January of 1917, attendances were low due to the weather and illness. At one time only 83 were present out of a total of 153.

27 June 1917: *The attendance has been very low all day. A great many children are absent at a Rechabite Demonstration in Aldershot.* (For those who don't know, Rechabites are a total abstinence Friendly Society founded in 1835.

12 Jan 1918: *Heavy fall of snow. 75 present.*

11 July 1918: *Mr. Arthy called to say that the school was to be closed for three weeks owing to mumps.*

10 Sep 1918: *School closed this afternoon as the children are going blackberrying for the Government.* (Perhaps the Prime Minister made jam!).

CAMBERLEY INFANTS SCHOOL

Jan 1914: *Poor attendance due to coughs and colds, also the mixed school still closed for building operations to proceed.*

6 March 1914: *Messrs. Martin, Tucker and Doman called with reference to new desks on order.*

7 July 1914: *Sent Millicent Cox by Miss Brooks to be inspected by Dr. Cadell who reported her to be suffering with measles. Sent her home immediately.*

10 July 1914: *Received 13 dual desks for Standard 1.*

31 August 1914: *Miss Constance Filimore commenced work here this morning in the place of Miss Beech who had left for New York 21 July 1914.*

12 April 1915: *Admitted 11 new scholars. Whooping cough still prevalent.*

On account of the influenza epidemic, the Camberley and Yorktown Council Schools had been closed for nearly a fortnight on Monday last, on which day they were to have re-opened. On the advice of Dr. Nevil P. Cadell, Medical Officer of Health for the Frimley District, it has been decided to keep the schools closed for another fortnight, and, as at present arranged, they will re-open on Monday, the 25th inst.

2 July 1915: *Wrote to Mr. Kennett calling his attention to the dangerous condition of the floorboards near outer door.*

The following week a half-day holiday was granted on account of a Sunday School Treat.

8 Nov 1915: *Closed this morning until after Christmas by order of Medical Officer, measles being very severe.*

8 Feb. 1916: *Owing to an exceptionally heavy snow storm only 63 out of 149 children presented themselves at school this morning. The socks and stockings of many of these children were in a very wet condition, necessitating attention, so no registers were marked.*

19 June 1916: Reopened this morning after Whitsun Holiday with an exceptional attendance, there being only 3 children absent.

14 Dec. 1916: *Closed this morning for the Christmas vacation, there being about 50% of the children absent with influenza.*

19 July 1917: *Mr. Arthy called and requested that in the event of injury to children through an air raid, Dr. Cadell be sent for.*

The staff at this time were Miss Newsome, Miss Filimore, Miss Ellis and Miss Brooks.

31 May 1918: *The attendance this week has been much affected by an outbreak of mumps. 117 present out of a total on the roll of 147.*

In 1962 this school amalgamated with the Junior School to form Camberley County Primary School. Mr. McNeal was the headmaster. He was my headmaster when I went to this school and no doubt remembers my rear view well—he hit it often enough with the cane. He died recently and must have been well known by many old Camberley school children.

CAMBERLEY MIXED SCHOOL

The headmaster Mr. E.V. Mellon was appointed on 24th August 1897 and stayed until 1921.

19 Jan 1914: *School reopened this morning. The work of enlargement is still far from completion. St. Georges Room still being maintained.*

9 Feb 1914: *New classrooms opened, St. Georges Room*

---

now not used. Playground space is still quite inadequate for the requirements of drill and play.

3 April 1914: *Average for the week 246 out of 285. The attendance is still very unsatisfactory. There is much sickness and fresh cases of measles.*

14 May 1914: *Two new garden spades and two forks received.*

22 May 1914: *Mr. A.E. Burgess visited the school gardens.*

12 June 1914: *Estimate for expenditure 1914/15–£53.18s.6d. on books and needlework material and £2.15s.7d. on prizes. I don't think that amount would last long these days, probably cover the cost of a spade and fork perhaps!*

6 July 1914: *Case of Raymond Bath was reported as suffering from scarlet fever by the Sanitary Inspector. Whole school fumigated.*

7 Sep 1914: *Mr. F.G. Grice ceased work today in order to join Lord Kitchener's army now actively recruiting.*

9 Oct 1914: *School prize giving. Donald Wallace, Mary Copsey, John Cox and Doris Crosby were winners. Also Stanley Sharman and Elsie Larne.*

23 Oct. 1914: *260 on the books. The work generally is making steady progress. The Head teacher, however finds with the shortage in staff, it difficult to give much attention to weaknesses evident in certain standards.*

6 Nov 1914: *The sum of 13 shillings collected and forwarded to the County War Relief Funds.*

18 Dec 1914: Headmaster's entry: *The examinations are now completed. The absence of the two efficient men teachers of the staff who have joined the Army has undoubtedly affected the success of the term's work. The young inexperienced members of the staff too readily become talkers instead of teachers, saying much but leaving only vague and ill-assimilated facts in the minds of the scholars.*

28 Jan 1915: *Orders received from the Chief Constable that the windows of the school are to be darkened when classes are held in the evening. There are fears of a German Zeppelin raid.*

16 Feb 1915: *Mr. C. Hicks, 73 Park Street, employed to assist in school garden 1/6d. an hour for 2½ hours a week (2 lessons).*

6 May 1915: *The instructor of the woodwork class considers that the defective eyesight of Cecil Pollard makes the handling of edged tools a source of danger to the lad. He will therefore be withdrawn from the class.*

21 May 1915: *Major General Bland Strange addressed the school this afternoon. Hall prettily decorated. Patriotic songs and a recitation given.* (Those were the days).

18 June 1915: *Centenary of the Battle of Waterloo. Special lesson given to the Senior Division reproduced afterwards as a composition exercise. 296 on books.*

27 Sept 1915: *Sangers Circus visited town. About 50 children absented themselves to see the afternoon per-*

formance. *Difficulty re no men teachers. Adjustment of timetables.*

8 Feb 1916: *Mr. Burgess visited and advised the formation of a ten plot school garden with two boys to each. 259 on books.*

19 June 1916: With Mr. Mellon the headteacher, there were now five women teachers—Misses Cocks, Neville, Pink, Rosewane and Thick. *No reading books, text books, pictures, maps, diagrams, science apparatus, chemicals or paints until further notice. No more than two-thirds of normal quantity will be supplied. No wood can be supplied nor school furniture.*

26 July 1916: *Miss E.G. Neville, for nearly five years a much esteemed and valuable member of the staff is leaving to get married. The school presented her with a silver-plated epergne.* (I had to look that up in a dictionary and found it to be an ornamental stand for a large dish or the centre of a table).

13 Oct. 1916: *An old scholar, Ernest West now serving in the Royal Fusiliers has won the Military Medal.*

20 Oct. 1916: *Tomorrow being Trafalgar Day, a special lesson on the importance of Britain's sea power was given to the Upper Classes today.*

27 Nov. 1916: *Cocoa is daily supplied to children who stay to dinner.*

14 Dec. 1916: *As the school is still without any heat, while the cold is extreme and sickness has considerably reduced the number, the M of H has ordered the closing of the school one week earlier than usual.*

6 March 1917: *Manure to the value of 10 shillings purchased for the school garden.*

12 June 1917: *H. Long found to be suffering from ringworm and at once excluded.*

5 July 1917: *AIR RAIDS–In case of a raid the Managers recommend:*
1) If official warning be given, dismiss children.
2) If no official warning, keep children in classrooms and lock gates.

5 Oct 1917: *A number of children have recently been admitted who have fled from London owing to the frequency and destructiveness of enemy air raids. 279 on books.*

20 Dec 1917: *All the paper boys absent this morning through non-arrival of papers.*

The next day a presentation of a carriage clock was made to Miss Cocks, as a tribute of esteem for her many hours of good work in the school.

1 Feb 1918: *A large number of attendances, nearly 140 have been cost this week through the lateness of the newspaper trains.*

27 Feb 1918: *Candidates for scholarship–Raymond Hardwell, Jessie Simmons, Fred Thomson*, Maud Urch.*

15 April 1918: *In the place of the geography lesson in the senior division an 'old boy', Warrant Officer Hy Tomms for three years resident in Singapore, gave an interesting account of his experiences in that town.*

2 July 1918: *Fred Thompson granted a junior teaching scholarship.*

9 Sept. 1918: *Standards 4 and 5 and part 6 and 7 went blackberrying with their teachers as per regulations. They gathered 4lbs. and the proceeds (3d. per lb) were given by the children to the Red Cross Fund.*

11 Sept. 1918: *Senior girls gathered blackberries 25lbs.*

29 Oct. 1918: *Attendance falling rapidly owing to Spanish Influenza. The chairman visited and on advice of the M of H closed the school.*

11 Nov 1918: *This morning news arrived of the virtual ending of the Great War by the signing of the Armistice.*

Mr. Mellon made a list of staff and pupils who lost their lives in the War, and also of those who were decorated.

Decorated:

Ernest West, *Royal Fusiliers, MM Sept. 1916*
Ernest Sharpe, *The Queens, MM Nov 1916*
George Pike, *Royal Fusiliers, MM Sept. 1917*
Reginald Cobbett, *The Queens, MM Nov. 1917*
Osbert Jackman, *Rifle Brigade, MM Nov 1918†*

Staff:

Alfred Wickes, *Quarter Master Sgt. 29th London Reg.*
A.H. Heachy, *Lt. 5th Dublin Fusiliers, Military Cross*
S.G. Wells, *Major Northern Fusiliers* (wounded)
E.F. Bristow, Lt. (wounded)
H.E. Merritt, (killed)
F.G. Price, *Quarter Master Sgt. East Kents*
J.F. Cross, *Staff Sgt.*
R.H. Powell, *Captain* (badly wounded)
S. Loveridge
Fred Butler, (killed 1917). Portrait hangs in school hall††
W.A. James, *A/Capt. and Adjudant (Salonica), France, Belgium and Salonica 1914/1919*

The Great War 1914-1918

The following old boys of the school gave their lives for their country:
James Nicklinson in retreat from Mons
Robert Harrington

Harry Carney Sgt.
Fred Godwin May 1915 Festuberg The Queens R.W.S.
Sydney Smith Sgt. Jan 1916
Reginald Cooper L.Cpl. killed at Loos 25 Sept. 1915
George Coe
Charles Baker RCA
George Bracknell Australian Contingent Sept. 1916
Joseph Jacobs 2nd Hampshire, Dardenelles 7/1/16
Harry Godwin
Edward Lacey RHA
Fred Ellis L Cpl (Portesbery Road) Royal Berks Reg 25/9/16
Chas West Sgt RW Kent
Charles Coe
William Steed
WT Thomas 19th Canadians 9/4/17
W. Faggetter
Chas Cook Sgt. July 1917
Victor Jackman Sept. 1917
Sidney Woodley Oct 1917, Nova Scotia Machine Gunners
Victor Emmings Nov 1917
Joseph Dale Sept. 1918
Fred Frankum, Sept 1918
Arthur Cooke, Sept. 1918
Arthur E. Eusor, Oct 1917, 102 Machine Gun Corps
Lt. Osbert Jackman
Sidney G.H. Pobgee, Corp 16th Lancers
Fred Mace
Lt. Scott, April 1918

There were some other names but the writing was not very clear so that this is not a complete list but an attempt by Mr. Mellon to ensure that the old boys and members of the staff would not be forgotten, and they certainly are not.

Looking through the old registers it was interesting to note the reasons for children leaving the school, remembering that the school leaving age was 14 years. 'Left district'; '14 years'; 'Private tuition'; 'gone on a visit', 'removal to Sandhurst', 'Labour certificate' or 'returned home'.

†See chapter on Gallantry Awards.

††As yet, I have been unable to discover the present whereabouts of the portrait of Fred Butler, perhaps someone can tell me.

*Fred Thompson was appointed Assistant Teacher at the school from 31 August 1931 and was my teacher when I went there. He is still around, and even today I feel uneasy when I see him. He was a dab hand at throwing lumps of chalk if you were not paying attention. I learned to duck at a very early age, thanks to him. I know he taught a great many local children and if they are like me, they really enjoyed it at school, thanks to teachers like him.

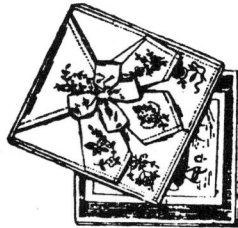

28

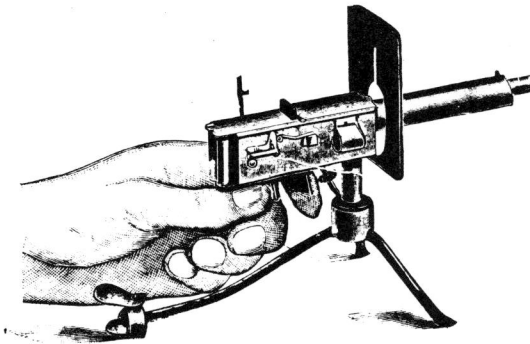

HAVING LOOKED at various aspects of Camberley during this period, I though it might be interesting to take a look at each year briefly to try to give some idea of what was happening and what was making the news. The incidents I quote are sometimes trivial and light-hearted, and sometimes of a more serious nature, especially those connected with the War, which of course dominated the newspapers during this period.

1914

On New Year's Day 1914 the opening of Camberley Heath Golf Club was the main story, the first ball being hit by His Highness Prince Christian of Schlesswig Holstein who was married to Helena August Victoria, daughter of Queen Victoria. They were married at Windsor Castle on 5th July 1866. Walter Toogood was the club professional at the time and took part in a foursome to open the Course.

In the Council Chamber a long discussion took place over a fire in Frimley where difficulty was experienced in obtaining water to douse it. It later transpired the cap was not taken off the fire hydrant. They also had trouble with the horses as the regular driver was unavailable, but even with these problems, they were at the fire within 50 minutes of the alarm being raised. Imagine that today, your house on fire and you have to wait 50 minutes for the fire engine!

In February a letter was published asking supporters of Camberley Football Club to be well behaved as twice that season the club had got into trouble on this count. The club was at the top of the West Surrey League at the time and as the forthcoming fixture was a cup game, permission had been given to charge admission—4d for men, free for women and children. If purchased before the day the ticket would be 3d.

In April the rates were 1s 4d. in the £. (Quite acceptable weren't they?). Also that month an article appeared in *The Statesman and Friend of India* which promoted Camberley as *the* place to live.

"*For the majority of time-expired workers from India, the question of where to settle in the Homeland presents formidable difficulties; and as they cannot afford to throw away many of their remaining previous years of life in sampling different locations for themselves they have generally to make up their minds on very insufficient information, the result usually being unsatisfactory... To testimonies of this kind I would add my own in favour of Camberley in Surrey. Situated on the north west border of Surrey, in the heart of the pine country between Bagshot and Farnborough, Camberley occupies the highest point in the neighbourhood. For miles around there stretches a glorious expanse of hilly country, partly covered with pines, partly consisting of gorse and heather-clad common. The variety of walks and rides is infinite and it is impossible to exhaust*

SUMMARY OF YEARS 1914-1918

the charms of the scenery which unfold themselves in every direction.

Unlike the majority of modern residential neighbourhoods, an attractive feature of the Camberley houses is that the grounds attached to them are unusually spacious."

It then goes on to extol the value of the railway service and the better private schools in the area, and finishes up by saying "*...Altogether Camberley is a place hard to beat for those who are in doubt where to set up their household goods on retirement from India and only needs to be better known to be very largely patronised.*" Would they say that today?

In June, North, South, West and East Streets were to become Brook Road, Oakley Road, Burford Road and Maitland Road respectively. By the following month 'Maitland Road' was not acceptable to the residents who wanted it changed to 'Queens Road'.

By August it was announced that all railway bridges and the railway would be protected and looked after by the police and the street lights would be allowed to burn all night. During this month many horses were requisitioned by the Military.

Also in August the results of a traffic census was published, it covered a period of seven days in three locations:

Camberley Traffic Census 1914

	Cycles	Motor Vehicles	Horse Drawn Vehicles	Horses & Cattle
High Street	15,782	2,842	3,124	4,225
Church Hill	3,824	1,406	1,334	1,620
Chobham Road	2,083	739	692	1,087

At the same time the Drill Hall was accepting recruits which were needed in all departments. By September, over 200 men had been recruited from Camberley. They were all sent to the Guildford Depot and then sent on their way by crowds of people singing patriotic songs.

Included in the sports column of the *Camberley News* was an article about footballers and the war: "*... But the competitions and the clubs all recognise that the Empire comes first and that it is the business of footballers in common with everyone else to do their best to see that Kaiser Wilhelm is not going to referee everything and everybody.*" Well said!

There was a letter from a Mr. W.R. Davies "Kingsclere", Camberley, asking for at least 100 local people to enrol in the Army to form a Camberley Company. "*Will 100 of you enrol by Monday next. We can then meet at the Drill Hall. Let Kipling's great words enspire us all:*

> *Comfort content delight*
> *The ages slow bought gain*
> *They shrivelled in a night*
> *Only ourselves remain*
> *to face the naked days*
> *In silent fortitude*
> *Through perils and dismay*
> *Renewed and renewed.*"

In October, P.C. Stevens, who prior to the war had been stationed at Camberley, arrived at the Bristol Infirmary, a victim of "white flag treachery". His letters speak for themselves. In one to a fellow police officer at Camberley he says, "*I was jolly lucky to get back to England again as we started attacking at 3.30 am on the 14th inst. and at 6 o'clock a party of Germans (about 150) surrendered to us under the white flag and then, when we had them formed up, they fired shrapnel shells amongst us. The first one grazed my throat and the second blew my rifle and the German's off my shoulder. It took my hat off and the bullet went right through my arm. Talk about a sight. All of them falling round me dead and wounded. The next thing when we got to hospital they started shelling so that we had to move again. Whilst I was going up the road with the other wounded I heard someone shout, 'Hello Billy,' and looking round I saw Charlie with a motor car. I can tell you, I had a proper shock seeing him out there. But I can't tell you what I said to him as I don't remember much as I was a bit lightheaded as it was terrible to have a piece out of your arm, but I'm all right now and am going to ask for 14 days leave when I get out of here before I go to the front again.*" In another letter to Sergeant Kenward he described having 10 hours of sleep in a week and having to march 23 miles a day with a full pack and 250 rounds of ammunition.

Later in the year there was a suggestion by Mr. Ashton of Yorktown School, and Mr. Mellon of the Camberley Schools for names of old boys serving in the War so that Rolls of Honour could be made for the schools.

There was a long report in the paper about a fatal accident that happened in Frimley Green when a traction engine, towing two trucks loaded with timber pulled over to allow a car to pass, and knocked down a Mrs. Chalcraft. She was treated on the spot, but died later at the old Cottage Hospital.

1914 started off quite normally, but ended with lots of the young men of the town going to do their duty in France in the trenches. For the next four years, life was not the same and many families had to live with the uncertainty of not knowing whether they would see their menfolk again.

1915

In February it was announced that since the recruiting office had opened in the High Street in November 1914, 102 men had enlisted, all for the Regular Army. In the following month at a Council Meeting it was proposed that it was not right to celebrate Empire Day in the usual way, although there might be some recognition of the day in the local schools. Admiral Johnstone said that to hold a celebration would be quite out of place. The West Surrey Horticultural Society Annual Show and the Rayner and Wright Football Cups were also cancelled.

The Post Office announced that arrangements were being made so that all Post Offices would accept French franc notes, each franc would be worth 9½d.

A romantic wedding took place in St. John's English Church in Boulogne France between Miss Kay Try of Camberley and Mr. T. North who was serving with the British Expeditionary Force. He was granted 48 hours leave but was unable to come to England. He met the bride and her party on the dockside and within the hour they were married. The wedding breakfast took place at the Hotel Du Porte. A few hours later the groom was on his way back to the front and his wife was on her way back to Camberley.

Both local schools had appealed to all of their past pupils who were serving in the the forces to contact them and reported that they had received letters from all over the world from 'old boys'.

The *Camberley News* 17th April printed a poem by Driver J. Crow, Royal Field Artillery, entitled '*Chums*'.

> *Three, what care we*
> *Jack Jock and Bill,*
> *All alive still.*
> *Shrapnell shell bursting like hell*
> *At gallop and run we've chased the hun.*
> *British made charms comrades in arms.*
> *Now horses we love a gift from above.*
> *They love us we know, we trust them and so*
> *We find in the end a horse, the soldier's best friend.*

And still on the subject of horses, the local Council were trying to decide if horses or motor vehicles were the best investment for the future. It was all over some stone chippings which Mr. Harry Doman (who else) thought would be better placed by being taken to where they were needed, and not dumped in the London Road first. Seeing as how the Council were paying so much for horse hire, shouldn't they go in for motor power? Many businesses were and he would bring it up at the next meeting of the Highways Committee.

The following letter appeared in May in the *Camberley News*:

"*Sir, I am the only German in Camberley at the present time. May I express my horror and disgust at the murder of innocent men, women and children by the sinking of the 'Lusitania'. I have been treated during the war with every consideration in Camberley and I want the people here to know that I at least condemn all these acts—poisonous gas, ill-treatment and shooting of prisoners—in the strongest terms. Yours Baron W Von Kamecke, 'Home Lodge', Connaught Road, Camberley.*

By 12th June it was announced that 232 recruits had been enlisted for the new army via the Recruiting Office in the High Street.

At a Council Meeting in July, Harry Doman suggested that policemen on traffic duty ought to have some protection and be in shelters. "In America the police have sunshades." This was met with laughter. He gave the chairman an illustration to be handed over to the right quarters.

There was a lovely little story about a Cove Parish Council member who on passing a railway bridge which was under guard, was challenged by a sentry. Having answered 'friend' on three occasions, he was surprised to find a bayonet close to his waistcoat. He took the matter up with the colonel who told him that the sentry had orders to challenge and if after the third challenge, he received no reply, he was to shoot or he would be liable to face a court martial. Two women, when challenged, had replied 'German spy' and the next time they did this, they were to be arrested and handed over to the police, to whom they would have to prove their innocence! (Now there's a warning!).

The *Camberley News* of 14th August reported that Baron Von Kamecke had been interned in the north of England. According to the newspaper report he had at one time been a Major in the Prussian Imperial Guard, then a military attaché in Washington and had lived in England for 20 years. The following week a letter was printed from his wife, denying he had ever been to America and stating he had been in the company guarding the old Empress, attaining the rank of Lieutenant.

In December 1915 there was a football match between W Rumble XI and Royal Aircraft Factory XI to raise money for the Cottage Hospital Fund.

1916

This year was again very much dominated by the War and the pages of the *Camberley News* did not contain much else.

I say that, yet one of the first bits of news concerned the making of marmalade. "*If everyone who is making marmalade will spare one pot for Camberley Military Hospitals the gift will be much appreciated by the patients.*" There were three such places in Camberley, one of which remains today. They were "Durley", Upper Park Road, "Firlands", where Firlands Avenue is now, and a house

Heatherbank, Church Hill, Camberley

called "Heatherbank" Church Hill which is still in existence.

Early in 1916 the local Tribunal met and considered claims for exemption from military service from a number of men. Some were allowed temporary exemption to sell a business or carry on working in essential jobs. There were some conscientious objectors who appealed against the decision of the local Tribunal to make them do military service.

On 15th April the whole of the back page was devoted to an article by a Mr. Younger concerning the treatment of our boys by the Germans. He was chairman of a committee who had examined the conditions in Germany. There were reports of Germans jeering at the dead, appalling conditions, no bedding facilities, no interest shown in the soldiers' injuries, and so on.

That same month, a letter from Private F. Tomms from 'somewhere in France' was printed in the *Camberley News*. It was written to the people of Camberley in general.

"*I write on behalf of the Camberley heads in the firing line in France. We often have the local paper sent out to us and are greatly interested in the goings on of late re the Tribunal matters. I recollect once several of us Camberley boys gathered in a dug-out in the firing line talking about the old times at home. One of the Company would say 'what about the Carnival?', another saying 'how about going down to the Rec, being early closing day there's sure to be some nice girls for a dance when the band strikes up.' In the middle of these conversations we are brought back to the reality of things by the bursting of a shell close by, or by the Sgt. shouting 'Stand to'. We then have to jump onto the first step and await orders. We are all anxiously looking forward to the end of the War and getting back to the dear old spot again. You may rely upon the Camberley Boys to do their best and to keep smiling. At present I am at the Base Camp having been in hospital. With best wishes to all readers.*" (I like that—don't you?)

On 13th May there was an announcement that the Post Office would now only be open from 9am until 7pm. Prior to this it had been opened from 8am until 8pm.

That month the Empress Eugenie who was born on 5th May 1826 celebrated her 90th birthday. She lived at Farnborough Hill and was visited by the Prince and Princess Napoleon.

In June at a house called "Conewood", a holiday creche for London children under five was opened by Viscountess Helmsley. It was described as a 'joyland for London children'. The house had been well adapted and was loaned by William Watson of Ascot for three months. Camberley had been chosen as it was a healthy place in the middle of pine forests. The creche was visited two months later by Princess Alexander of Teck, who motored down to Camberley and had lunch with Mr. and Mrs. Francis Brenton at "Ravenswood". At the house she complimented Supt. Burn on the smartness of the guard of honour from the Royal Albert Orphan Asylum.

In July 1916 Colonel Sir Arthur Hammond suggested that a small obelisk be erected after the War as a tribute to all those who had fallen or would fall in the War.

In August the Council appealed to relatives of men lost in the War to send them details so if it was decided to erect a memorial, they would have all the necessary details.

In the Camberley News of 9th December, Harry Doman was still on about shelters for policemen on point duty. He thought it was a disgrace to the county to see police standing directing traffic in appalling weather conditions. The A.A. provided shelters for their men, so why not the police? He suggested a revolving sentry box which they could rotate in each direction, and on this subject he felt they should write to the County Council. As nobody seconded this the chairman, Major General Dalrymple remarked, *"I should like a resolution that some of our young policemen take their places in the Army – they won't get any shelters there!"* (Shame, I would have liked a rotating shelter).

In December the Frimley and Camberley War Depot at "Kingsclear" announced there had been 3,824 working attendances. 14,189 articles had been made and sent out to 51 destinations.

1917

The year started, as did the previous two, with reports in the paper of the deaths of local youths in the War, and court cases. Food was not as plentiful as before. By March it was announced that the local bakers would only bake on Mondays, Tuesdays, Thursdays and Saturdays. A shortage of potatoes in the town was beginning to be noticed. Some shops were limiting their customers to 2lb each, while one shop in Yorktown displayed the notice 'No potatoes this weekend'. The vegetable carts that normally toured the town were similarly affected.

In the following month the rates for the half year had increased from 1s 4d to 1s 6d.

I noticed that on the back of the Camberley News was a column entitled "Hints for Allotment Holders" by Spade-worker. Also the War Agricultural Committee announced that Mr. Crosby would visit each allotment on Wednesdays and Fridays between 6pm and 9pm to give instruction and advice. Places visited on a fortnightly rota were in Park Street, France Hill Estate, Frimley Road, Harcourt House, Cromwell Road, Mr. Kennett's land, Roscommon and Portesbury Road.

On 1st April the recruiting office in the High Street closed down. The Roll of Honour had been transferred to the Municipal Offices for safekeeping. (I wonder where it is now?)

The Camberley News in July contained a wonderful piece of information that if the hair on the heads of the people in the U.K. were put into one strand it would total 760 million miles, enough to link the Earth and the Sun by eight strands. (I bet you didn't know that, did you?)

On August 18th, Bronco Bill's Circus came to town and was sited in Mr. Doman's meadow off the Frimley Road. It had seating for 5,000 people and every comfort for the visitor. There were whipcrackers, lasso artists and bronco acts to be seen. The highlight of the show was the "Attack on the Deadwood Stage."

That month saw the arrival of the first gas driven car in Aldershot—a Studabaker 15/20 HP car arrived at the Aldershot Gas Water and Lighting Office in Victoria Road with a canvas container in a wooden frame on its roof. This could hold 220 cubic feet of gas, enough for a trip of 12-14 miles. A trial run of 12 miles was made before it returned to be refilled from a 2 inch pipe, which took 10 minutes. The car was owned by Mr. Brandon the tobacco grower from Cookham and driven by Mr. F.J. Barnwell.

In September the St. Michael's Social Club which met at their hall in The Avenue, announced that from the start of that year's football season they had reformed their team, the average age would be 18 years. They intended to play their matches at the London Road Recreation Ground.

The District Rate was to be unchanged at 1s 6d. in the pound.

Although still in the middle of the War, the Council were discussing the road construction programme and were looking at estimates of costs for certain roads in the area. The re-construction work of Lake and Wharf Road in Mytchett, Frimley Green Road, Deepcut Road and Chobham Road had been estimated at £10,422, the actual cost was £12,198 17s 9d. The cost on the rates was 2/6d. in the pound for the next five years. The Chairman remarked on how fortunate they were to have such good roads as they had, and at a comparitively cheap cost.

Well, that was the highlights of 1917 in Camberley, so now let's go on to the final year of the War—one which started in the usual way, but which ended, for many people in Camberley, on a far happier note.

1918

Let me start this year off with a small footnote that appeared in the Camberley News. *"The men of the Empire are laying down their lives in battle, the women cannot do less than help in the great task of feeding the Country and helping the men at the front. Saving the food means feeding the guns."*

In April Admiral Johnstone was asking local people to grow more potatoes as the Government were daily urging people to do so. A million acres needed to be planted this year and Surrey was not as far forward as it could be. He appealed for women to club together to look after a ten rod plot. If applications were made either to the Admiral or to Mr. Robinson in the High Street, then the Food Products Committee would do all they could to get round to them. It ended up by saying *"This is most urgent. Think of the German danger threatening us."*

In the Camberley News 27th April, most of the front page was devoted to the fact that the following week was to be 'Aeroplane Week', and Camberley needed to raise £35,000. Such headlines as 'AEROPLANES TO WIN THE WAR' and 'CAVALRY OF THE AIR' were included. During the first half week £18,000 was raised; a tremendous achievement for the town. At the end of the week a grand total of £55,243 16s 6d. had been raised which surprised many people who had doubted the Committee would raise even £20,000. The Chairman was a Mr. W.R. Davies who lived at 'Kingsclear'.

In July, Admiral Johnstone agreed to become President of a newly formed Rabbit Club, the aim of which was to increase meat production and form a national rabbit industry. In Camberley it would cover Frimley, Bagshot, and Windlesham. Other committee members included Mr. Frederic Robinson and Mr. W.R. Davies. By September it had 34 members and five proposed new members.

In August, Frimley Park was sold through Sadler and Baker to Mr. Berry of Leeds. It included some 127 acres of land altogether, and was built about 1670. The present King of Siam had also lived there.

In October the rates were reduced to 1s. 4d in the pound.

November 16th issue of the Camberley News contained news of how people in the Frimley and Camberley area received news of the armistice. Lots of bunting and flags around and the promise of festivities to be arranged at a later date. What a relief that must have been to all those back home. The women could now look forward to the return of their menfolk and start to plan a new life. Of course, how Camberley changed after the War and beyond is another story, or even perhaps another book... who knows?

Most leisure time activities were suspended during the war so entertainment chiefly consisted of a visit to the cinema, or as a treat, the Hippodrome theatre in Aldershot where such top class performers as Jack Hulbert, Cicely Courtneidge and Harry Champion appeared.

The cinemas showed films such as Charlie Chaplin, and of course, the newsreels showed the fighting at the front.

The Electric Theatre: Opened in 1910, was situated in the premises now occupied by *Camberley Toys* in the High Street.

THE WORLD'S 60 BEST DESSERTS...
PERIOD.
DAVID COURTEAU

PHOTOGRAPHER: Antoine Sicotte
ART DIRECTORS: Antoine Sicotte & Véronique Paradis
GRAPHIC DESIGNER: Laurie Auger
COVER DESIGNER: Laurie Auger
FOOD STYLIST: Véronique Paradis & David Courteau
ENGLISH TRANSLATOR: Lorien Jones
COPY EDITOR: Anna Phelan

PROJECT EDITOR: Antoine Ross Trempe

ISBN: 978-2-924155-06-6

©2013, CARDINAL PUBLISHERS / LES ÉDITIONS CARDINAL
All rights reserved.

Legal Deposit: 2013
Bibliothèque et Archives du Québec
Library and Archives Canada
ISBN: 978-2-924155-06-6

The publisher acknowledges the financial support of the Government of Canada through the Canada Book Fund (CBF) for its publishing activities and the support of the Government of Quebec through the tax credits for book publishing program (SODEC).

Originally published under the title
"Les 60 meilleurs desserts du monde... Point final."

PRINTED IN CANADA

Discover our upcoming books and much more!
WWW.FACEBOOK.COM/THEWORLDS60BEST

THE WORLD'S 60 BEST

DESSERTS

PERIOD.

THE WORLD'S ✹60✹ BEST

DESSERTS

PERIOD.

ABOUT THIS BOOK

The 60 desserts in this book are, *in our opinion*, the 60 best desserts in the world. Our team of chefs, writers, and foodies explored everything the culinary world has to offer to create this collection of the world's 60 best desserts.

We based our recipes on the following criteria:

QUALITY OF INGREDIENTS
ORIGINALITY
TASTE
APPEARANCE
SIMPLICITY

Are these our personal favorite desserts? Of course! But rest assured, our team of passionate, dedicated gourmets put time and loving care into formulating and testing each recipe in order to provide you with the 60 best desserts ever. In fact, our chef brought each freshly made treat straight from the kitchen into the studio—no colorants, no sprays, no special effects added—and after each photo shoot, our creative team happily devoured the very desserts you see in these photos.

We hope you'll enjoy discovering these recipes and using this book as much as we enjoyed making it.

TABLE OF CONTENTS

CREDITS 002

ABOUT THIS BOOK 009

INTRO 017

FLAVOR & COST LEGEND 018

A SHORT HISTORY OF DESSERT 021

MUST-HAVE TOOLS 023

TIPS & TRICKS 025

HOW-TO GUIDE 027

GLOSSARY 029

THE CHEF'S SECRET 031

THE BEST BROWNIES EVER.................................032

AFTERNOON SNACK COOKIES..........................034

CLASSIC CHEESECAKE.....................................036

HOMEMADE FROZEN YOGURT..........................038

COCONUT SNOWBALLS.....................................040

POUND CAKE WITH LEMON GLAZE...................044

THE PUMPKIN PIE..046

SEXY RED VELVET..048

PORTUGUESE NATAS.......................................050

CARROT CAKE WITH CREAM CHEESE ICING.......052

HOLIDAY FRUITCAKE..056

KING CAKE...058

CREAMY HOT CHOCOLATE...............................060

THE LEMON MERINGUE PIE..............................062

CHIC CLAFOUTIS...064

THE CRÈME BRÛLÉE..068

PUMPKIN CREAM CANNOLI...............................070

GRANDMA'S APPLE PIE....................................072

TRUFFLES THREE WAYS....................................074

TROPICAL DELIGHT...076

TRIPLE CHOCOLATE COOKIES...........................080

FROZEN POP TRIO...082

SWEET PEAR & ALMOND TART..........................084

NOUGAT ICE CREAM.......................................086

CHOCO-CHERRY-CARAMEL CUPS......................088

BLUEBERRY CASHEW CHEESECAKE...................092

STICKY TOFFEE PUDDING.................................094

BAKLAVA...096

CHURROS..098

PECAN & BOURBON PIE...................................100

DOUBLE FRUIT CRISP......................................104

DOUGHNUTS..106

FRESH FRUIT TARTS..108

THE TIRAMISU..110

SUGAR PIE...112

SCONES & JAM..116

STRAWBERRIES & CHAMPAGNE.......................118

CHOCOLATE LAVA CAKES................................120

THE PARIS-BREST...122

OLD-FASHIONED STRAWBERRY SHORTCAKE.....124

KEY LIME PIE..128

FRENCH MILLE-FEUILLES.................................130

FRENCH CANADIAN "PUDDING CHÔMEUR".......132

MACARONS..134

LUSCIOUS LEMON CREAM CUPS.......................136

WHITE CHOCOLATE MACADAMIA COOKIES.......140

THE TARTE TATIN..142

GRILLED CHOCOLATE BANANAS.......................144

RUM BABAS...146

THE ICE CREAM SANDWICH.............................148

BISCOTTI & AFFOGATO....................................152

ROASTED PEACHES..154

COFFEE PANNA COTTA....................................156

YULE LOG..158

CRÊPES...160

NANAIMO BARS..164

CARAMEL BANANA CRUNCH PUDDING.............166

CITRUS SURPRISE...168

BREAD PUDDING & APPLE BUTTER....................170

CHOCOLATE POTS DE CRÈME..........................172

INGREDIENTS INDEX.......................................176

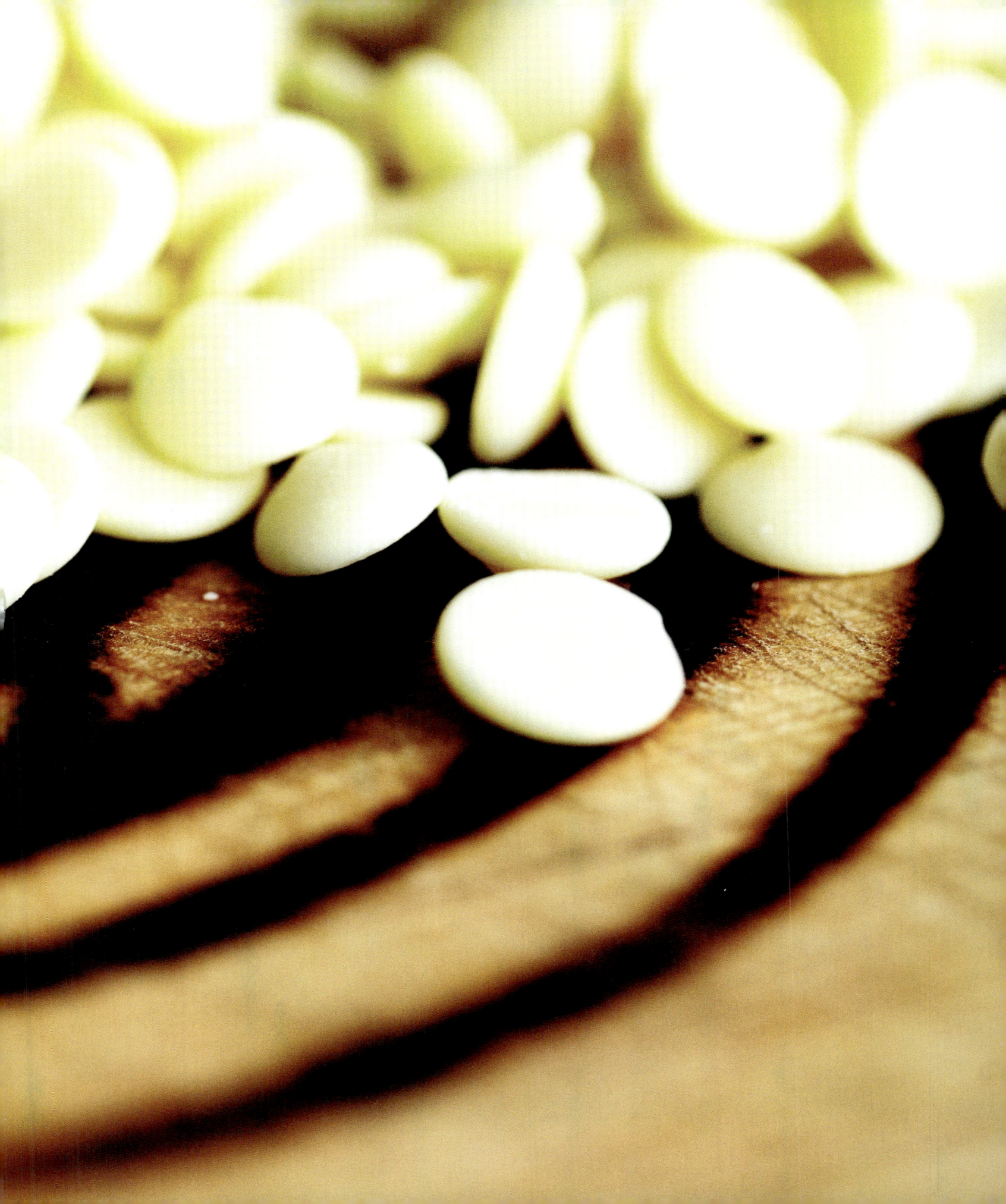

INTRO

Every one of the 60 best desserts in this book features a flavor and cost legend (see pages 018 and 019) to guide your taste buds as well as your wallet in choosing the perfect dish. You will also find a glossary of culinary terms (page 029), handy cooking tips and tricks (page 025), and a list of must-have kitchen tools (page 023) that will help you create the world's BEST desserts. Finally, use the easy-to-follow table of contents (pages 010 and 011) and ingredients index (pages 176 to 179) to find everything you're looking for.

Impress guests with your food knowledge from our informative "Did you know?" sidebars, and take your desserts to the next level thanks to our tasty tips and serving suggestions!

Bon appétit!

 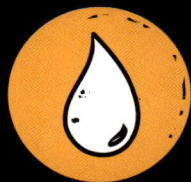  

SWEET   RICH DIFFICULTY COST

LEGEND

LEVEL OF SWEETNESS

🧁 LOW   🧁🧁 MEDIUM   🧁🧁🧁 HIGH

CREAMY • BUTTERY • LUSCIOUS

💧 LOW   💧💧 MEDIUM   💧💧💧 HIGH

LEVEL OF DIFFICULTY

👨‍🍳 LOW   👨‍🍳👨‍🍳 MEDIUM   👨‍🍳👨‍🍳👨‍🍳 HIGH

COST OF INGREDIENTS

🐷 LOW   🐷🐷 MEDIUM   🐷🐷🐷 HIGH

A SHORT HISTORY OF DESSERT

When you think of dessert, the first thing that comes to mind is, naturally, sugar! And yet, the very first desserts, as we know them today, were sweetened with fruit and honey: we know that ancient civilizations consumed dried fruits, nuts, and honeycomb. Cane sugar only appeared in Europe in the Middle Ages, and what's more, sweet dishes weren't always served at the end of a meal. What did conclude a meal wasn't necessarily sweet: the word dessert, after all, comes from the Old French *desservir*, which merely means "to un-serve."

Historically, sugar was used for medicinal purposes; apothecaries prepared pastilles and pastes with sugar to soothe problems of the stomach, bladder, and kidneys. Candied ginger, aniseed, and coriander were taken to "close" the stomach at the end of a meal, and to help with digestion. Prior to the 18th century, sugar used to sweeten food was a precious commodity, a luxury item available only to the very wealthy. Crusaders brought sugar home from the Holy Land, and Christopher Columbus sailed from the Canary Islands with cuttings of sugar cane, the first to reach the New World. By the 19th century, sugar production had hugely increased due to popular demand and advances in cultivation technology. In fact, the demand for sugar influenced the course of human history; it caused wars and perpetuated slavery, and brought about mass migrations and the formation of new colonies.

Desserts are constantly evolving as new techniques and ingredients are discovered and added. The first recipe for apple pie dates back to 1381, while the one of the earliest known recipes for ice cream comes from China, and dates back to around 200 BCE. These desserts probably wouldn't please our modern palates, as apple pie typically didn't contain any sugar, and the Chinese often made their ice cream with rice. But of course, as with most dishes, it is geography, tradition, and culture that set one dessert apart from another. Because of the globalization and accessibility of ingredients, traditional desserts of the world have become available across the globe, from baklava to churros to gelato to the celebrated all-American apple pie.

Over the centuries, dessert has changed from simple foods like nuts and fruit, to complicated layered cakes and delicate soufflés and mousses. Science and cooking go hand in hand, and pastry chefs and bakers are pushing the culinary boundaries now more than ever before. Who knows what the future holds for desserts? In the meantime, roll up your sleeves and get ready for the ultimate dessert experience with *The World's 60 Best Desserts... Period.*

MUST-HAVE TOOLS

FOR THE WORLD'S BEST DESSERTS

1. An **electric hand mixer** for beating, whipping, and creaming batters, doughs, icings, and more, to make the world's 60 best desserts

2. Or, if you plan to do a lot of baking, invest in a quality **stand mixer** to make the job even easier

3. A **rolling pin** for rolling out pie crust dough, puff pastry, etc.

4. **Tart molds** for making exquisite pies and tarts

5. A **springform pan** for easily removing cakes with delicate bottom layers, like cakes with graham cracker crusts

6. An **offset baker's spatula** for easy icing

7. A **fine wire mesh strainer** for sifting dry ingredients and for straining liquid mixtures

8. A **whisk** for whipping, beating, and mixing

9. A **pastry bag** for filling pastry, shaping dough and batter, and piping out icing and whipped cream to decorate cakes

10. A **flexible plastic spatula** for delicately folding ingredients together and for scraping out bowls

11. A **microplane grater** for grating citrus zest, spices, chocolate, etc.

12. A **silicone baking mat** or **parchment paper** for lining baking pans and sheets to prevent your desserts from sticking

13. A **baking sheet** for baking cookies, pastries, and other tempting treats

14. **Measuring cups and spoons** for measuring precise quantities

15. A **kitchen scale** for weighing ingredients and measuring the very precise quantities needed for true pastry magic to happen

TIPS & TRICKS

FOR CREATING THE WORLD'S BEST DESSERTS

1. Pastry making is an art that requires precision. Take the time to read and fully understand the recipe before starting, make sure to accurately measure the ingredients in advance, preheat the oven to the exact temperature, and follow the recipe to the letter. Just be confident, stay focused, and don't worry—your desserts are sure to be delectable.

2. Buy a candy thermometer that reaches 400 degrees Fahrenheit. Many recipes require sugar to be heated, and the temperature determines how the sugar will set as it cools to make different confections, from a simple syrup, to fudge, to hard candy. A thermometer will make sure all your recipes turn out perfectly!

3. Be very careful when making caramel! The sugar becomes extremely hot and might spatter, and remember to never, ever, test the temperature, or taste, by dipping your fingers into the caramel. Be careful when pouring it or adding other ingredients, and above all, enjoy it—once it's cooled down!

4. When you're ready to prepare your pastry, make a big batch. Divide it, wrap it, and freeze it in one-recipe portions. Both basic and sweet pie pastry keep wonderfully in the freezer for up to four months. Just defrost it in the refrigerator overnight, or at room temperature a few hours before making your dessert

5. It's best to use milk with a higher fat content—your desserts will be richer, creamier, and tastier.

6. Unsalted butter is a must for making pastry, even though salted butter is generally preferred for cooking. When buying butter, cut it into four equal portions, wrap them individually, and freeze. You'll have four ready-to-use 1/2-cup (120 g) portions. Remove the desired portions from the freezer well in advance and let sit until they reach the temperature listed in the recipe (cold, room temperature, etc.).

7. Sift the flour before adding the other ingredients. Flour easily absorbs moisture, and this step will prevent floury lumps in your confections.

8. The best type of gelatin for desserts is sheet gelatin, which can be found in most grocery stores and is very easy to prepare: just soak in cold water for a few minutes before adding it to the other ingredients in your recipe. When the sheets are soft, they're ready to use. Make sure to gently wring them dry before using.

9. Can't resist adding a personal touch to your desserts? It's important to follow the basic recipe very closely, but go ahead and try different types of chocolate, dried fruit, nuts, or fresh fruit. Even though precision is key when it comes to pastry, you can still get creative!

10. Finally, always remember that the best desserts are made using the freshest, highest quality ingredients.

HOW-TO GUIDE

PASTRY

FOR BASIC PIE PASTRY
Makes 3 portions

Ingredients
3-3/4 cups plus 1 tbsp (500 g) flour
1 tsp (5 g) salt
1 tbsp (15 g) sugar
1 cup (225 g) cold unsalted butter, cut into cubes
2/3 cup plus 2 tsp (170 g) milk
1 egg

Preparation
Sift flour, salt, and sugar together into a bowl. Add butter and, using your hands, mix pastry until it has the texture of coarse crumbs.

Using a whisk, combine milk and egg. Add to butter and dry ingredient mixture and knead just until it becomes a smooth pastry. Wrap dough and chill in the refrigerator for at least 1 hour.

FOR SWEET PIE PASTRY
Makes 4 portions

Ingredients
2 cups plus 4 tsp (500 g) unsalted butter, softened
2-1/3 cups (300 g) icing sugar
3 eggs
6 cups plus 1 tbsp (800 g) flour
1/2 tbsp (7-1/2 g) salt
1 cup (100 g) almond flour

Preparation
In a bowl, cream together butter and sugar. Add eggs and mix. Add flour, salt, and almond flour. Mix just until pastry is smooth; don't overmix. Wrap pastry and chill in the refrigerator for at least 1 hour.

MAKING THE PIE CRUST

Lightly flour a work surface and the bottom of the pastry. Using a rolling pin, roll out a portion of pastry dough, starting at the center and rolling out toward the edges, just until crust is about 1/8 inch thick. Add a bit of flour as needed to the dough, work surface, or rolling pin, to prevent it from sticking.

Brush excess flour off of pastry and roll around the rolling pin (this will make it easier to transfer it to the pie plate). Unroll crust into the pie plate, making sure there are no gaps that might let the filling escape. Trim excess pastry around the edges using a small knife or a pastry cutter.

PREBAKING THE PIE CRUST

Preheat oven to 350°F (175°C).

Line pie crust with parchment paper and fill with dried beans to add weight. Bake for 10 to 15 minutes, or until lightly golden. Remove from oven, let cool to room temperature, and remove beans.

GLOSSARY

1. SIFT

To put flour, sugar, or another dry ingredient through a sieve to remove lumps.

2. PEEL AND SEGMENT

To remove the peel, pith, and inner membranes of a citrus fruit, leaving only the pulp. The easiest way to peel and segment citrus fruit is to cut off both ends, place it on a flat work surface, and peel downwards, underneath the white pith, around the entire fruit.

3. FLOUR

To sprinkle a flat work surface or a baking pan with flour to prevent a dessert from sticking and make it easier to turn the item out of the pan.

4. WHIP

To vigorously beat a liquid, or a combination of liquids, until smooth. Whipping also incorporates air into a mixture (like whipped cream or meringue), making it light and fluffy.

5. ROLL OUT

To spread and flatten pastry or dough using a rolling pin. Lightly flour the work surface before rolling out your dough to prevent it from sticking.

6. ZEST

To remove the zest, or outer skin, of citrus fruits with a zester, grater, or peeling knife.

7. CREAM

To beat butter by hand, or using an electric mixer, until it becomes light and airy.

8. CARAMELIZE WITH A KITCHEN TORCH

To turn sugar into a caramel by heating it using a kitchen torch or a small blowtorch. Caramelizing turns meringue and sugar a beautiful golden brown color, and creates a crunchy layer on the top of crème brûlée. Be sure to keep the flame very low to prevent burning.

9. FOLD

To incorporate a delicate preparation into another by passing a spatula down through a mixture in a bowl, passing it across the bottom, and coming back up over top. This process is repeated until the ingredients are combined.

10. CHOP

To cut into small pieces with a sharp instrument (knife or food processor).

11. BAIN-MARIE

A water bath for melting or cooking food very slowly to prevent it from burning. Typically, a container holding the preparation is placed in another container holding the water bath.

12. PREBAKE

To bake an empty pie crust before filling it, which prevents pastry from getting soggy when the pie has a liquid or creamy filling. This step is also necessary when the filling doesn't need to be cooked.

THE PASTRY CHEF'S SECRET

To precisely measure quantities, and for the best results, pastry chefs use a kitchen scale to weigh their ingredients. Both traditional and digital scales are affordable and widely available.

As you will see, the ingredients in this book are measured by weight, using the metric system. Their volume equivalent, using the imperial system, is also provided, but should only be used as a guideline.

Weighing the ingredients is the best way to make the world's best desserts... period!

THE BEST BROWNIES EVER

MAKES 8 BROWNIES
PREP TIME: 45 MINUTES

TASTY TIP

Add a few small handfuls of chopped walnuts to your brownie batter for a crunchy version of this classic treat!

DID YOU KNOW?

A brownie is a dense, rich chocolate cake, but according to Scottish folklore, a brownie is also a diminutive elf-like creature that only comes out at night and helps with household tasks in exchange for food and small gifts. They are also thought to bring good luck!

INGREDIENTS

1 cup (150 g) dark chocolate, roughly chopped
1/2 cup (115 g) unsalted butter
2 eggs, beaten
1 cup plus 2 tbsp (225 g) sugar
1/4 tsp (1 g) salt
2/3 cup (100 g) flour, sifted

FOR CHOCOLATE SAUCE

3/4 cup (180 ml) 35% cream
1/2 cup (125 ml) milk
1 cup (150 g) dark chocolate, roughly chopped

PREPARATION

Preheat oven to 350°F (175°C).

Melt chocolate and butter in a bain-marie. Remove from heat and add eggs, sugar, salt, and flour, and mix well. Pour batter into a buttered 7-inch square baking pan.

Bake for 30 minutes, or until a toothpick inserted into the center comes out with a few moist crumbs attached, but not completely clean. The brownies should be soft in the middle and more cooked around the edges.

For chocolate sauce: In a pot, bring cream and milk to a boil. Put chocolate into a bowl and pour hot mixture over top. Whisk until smooth and creamy.

Serve brownies with your favorite ice cream, and top with chocolate sauce.

2

AFTERNOON SNACK COOKIES

MAKES 20 COOKIES
PREP TIME: 30 MINUTES

INGREDIENTS

3/4 cup (96 g) flour
1 tsp (5 g) baking powder
1/4 tsp (1 g) salt
1/2 cup (120 g) unsalted butter, softened
1 cup (230 g) brown sugar, lightly packed
1 tsp (5 ml) vanilla extract
1 egg
1-1/2 cups (185 g) rolled (old-fashioned) oats
1 cup (175 g) dried figs, diced

PREPARATION

Preheat oven to 350°F (175°C).

In a bowl, combine flour, baking powder, and salt. Set aside.

In another bowl, cream together butter, brown sugar, and vanilla extract. Add egg. Add dry ingredients, oats, and figs, and mix to combine; don't overmix.

Using spoons, shape dough into small balls (about 2 tbsp each) and drop onto a baking sheet lined with parchment paper, or a silicone baking mat.

Bake for 10 minutes, or until cookies are golden brown.

CLASSIC CHEESECAKE

3

MAKES 12 SERVINGS
PREP TIME: 1 HOUR

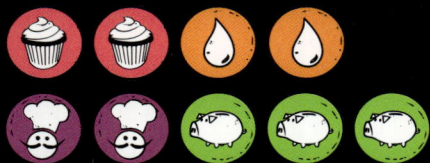

REST TIME: 4 HOURS

TASTY TIP

Replace the strawberry topping with caramel, or a purée made from your favorite fruit.

DID YOU KNOW?

During the first Olympic Games, the Ancient Greeks served cheesecake to the athletes to build up their energy!

FOR GRAHAM CRACKER CRUST

1 cup (90 g) graham cracker crumbs
1/3 cup (45 g) pecans, chopped
2 tbsp (26 g) sugar
1/3 cup (80 ml) butter, melted

FOR CHEESECAKE FILLING

3 packages (8 oz each) cream cheese, brought to room temperature
1 cup (200 g) sugar
3 eggs

FOR STRAWBERRY TOPPING

3 cups (450 g) fresh strawberries, washed, hulled, and halved or quartered
1/2 cup (100 g) sugar
1 tbsp (15 ml) lemon juice

PREPARATION

Preheat oven to 350°F (175°C).

For graham cracker crust: In a bowl, combine graham cracker crumbs, chopped pecans, sugar, and melted butter. Press mixture firmly into the bottom of an 8-inch a springform pan. Bake for 8 minutes and then let cool to room temperature.

For cheesecake filling: Using an electric mixer with the whisk attachment, beat together cream cheese and sugar. Add eggs one at a time, mixing well after each addition.

Pour into springform pan and bake, about 40 minutes. Cake should still be slightly jiggly in the center. Let cool completely and then chill in the refrigerator for at least 4 hours.

For strawberry topping: In a pot, combine strawberries, sugar, and lemon juice. Mix with a wooden spoon and cook for 10 minutes over low heat. Transfer to a bowl and chill in the refrigerator before spooning over top of cheesecake.

HOMEMADE FROZEN YOGURT

4

MAKES 4 CUPS
PREP TIME: 4 HOURS AND 30 MINUTES

INGREDIENTS

2 cups (200 g) fresh or frozen cranberries
4/5 cup (170 g) sugar
2 tbsp (30 ml) lemon juice
2 cups (500 ml) plain yogurt
3/4 cup (180 ml) 35% cream

PREPARATION

In a pot, bring cranberries, sugar, and lemon juice to a boil and let simmer until cranberries burst and are completely cooked.

Transfer mixture to a food processor; add yogurt and cream, and purée until smooth. Let cool completely in the refrigerator.

Transfer to an ice cream maker and freeze according to manufacturer's directions.

TASTY TIP

Instead of cranberries, make strawberry, raspberry, peach, mango, pear, or cherry frozen yogurt... or why not try a combination of your very favorite fruits?

5

COCONUT SNOWBALLS

MAKES 24 SNOWBALLS
PREP TIME: 2 HOURS AND 30 MINUTES

INGREDIENTS

4 egg whites
1 cup (200 g) sugar
3 cups (240 g) finely shredded unsweetened coconut
1 tsp (3 g) flour
1/2 tsp (2 ml) vanilla extract

PREPARATION

Preheat oven to 215°F (102°C).

In a bain-marie, heat egg whites and sugar together, whisking constantly, until mixture reaches a temperature of 122°F (50°C). Using a hand or stand mixer with the whisk attachment, mix at medium speed until mixture is cool and forms stiff peaks.

Using a flexible plastic spatula, fold in coconut, flour, and vanilla extract.

Using spoons, form into 1-1/2-inch balls and drop onto a baking sheet lined with parchment paper, or a silicone baking mat.

Bake for 2 hours.

POUND CAKE WITH LEMON GLAZE

MAKES 10 SERVINGS
PREP TIME: 50 MINUTES

TASTY TIP

The classic lemon pound cake is absolutely scrumptious, but it's also an extremely versatile dessert: orange, almond, and chocolate are all popular flavor variations!

DID YOU KNOW?

This cake was traditionally made with a pound each of flour, butter, sugar, and eggs.

FOR CAKE

1-3/4 cups (230 g) flour
1/2 tsp (2 g) salt
1/2 tsp (2 g) baking powder
2/3 cup (150 g) unsalted butter, softened
1-1/2 cups (300 g) sugar
Zest of 1/2 lemon
Seeds from 1 vanilla bean
3 eggs
1/2 cup plus 1 tbsp (150 g) sour cream

FOR ICING

1 tbsp (15 ml) lemon juice
1 cup (125 g) icing sugar

PREPARATION

For cake: Preheat oven to 350°F (175°C).

Butter a 4-inch x 9-inch loaf pan and line with parchment paper. Set aside.

Sift flour, salt, and baking powder into a bowl. Set aside.

Using a hand or stand mixer, cream together butter, sugar, lemon zest, and vanilla bean seeds. Add eggs one at a time, mixing after each addition. Add dry ingredients and sour cream at the same time and mix until blended. Pour batter into prepared loaf pan and bake for 40 minutes, or until a toothpick inserted into the center comes out clean.

For icing: Combine lemon juice and icing sugar. Mix until smooth and then chill in the refrigerator.

Remove cake from oven and spread icing over top. Slice and serve.

THE PUMPKIN PIE

SERVES 6
PREP TIME: 1 HOUR

FOR PUMPKIN PURÉE: 45 MINUTES

DID YOU KNOW?

Winter squash and pumpkin are often mistaken for each other, the latter being more common in North America and Asia. The pumpkin has a round shape and is orange in color, whereas the winter squash is more or less flat and, depending on the variety, varies from red to dark green in colour.

INGREDIENTS

1 pumpkin or 1-3/5 cups (425 g) store-bought canned pure pumpkin purée
3 eggs
1/2 cup (120 ml) 35% cream
1/2 cup (110 g) brown sugar, lightly packed
3/4 tsp (3 g) ground cinnamon
1/4 tsp (1 g) ground ginger
1/8 tsp (1/2 g) ground cloves
1/4 tsp (1 g) ground nutmeg
1/2 tsp (2 g) salt
1 portion basic pie pastry (see recipe on page 027)

PREPARATION

Preheat oven to 350°F (175°C).

To make your own pumpkin purée, cut a pumpkin in half, remove seeds, and place, cut sides down, on a baking sheet. Bake in a 350°F (175°C) oven for 40 minutes. Scoop out cooked pumpkin flesh, transfer to a food processor, and purée until smooth. Use 1-3/5 cups pumpkin purée to make the pie.

In a bowl, whisk together pumpkin pie filling ingredients. Pour into pie crust.

Bake for 35 to 40 minutes. Let cool to room temperature, and then chill in the refrigerator. Serve with whipped cream.

SEXY RED VELVET

SERVES 8
PREP TIME: 2 HOURS

FOR RED VELVET CAKE

1/2 cup (120 g) unsalted butter, softened
1-1/2 cups (300 g) sugar
2 eggs
1 bottle (60 ml) red food coloring
2 tsp (10 ml) vanilla extract
2-1/2 cups (375 g) flour, sifted
1 tbsp (8 g) cocoa powder
1 cup (250 ml) buttermilk
2 tsp (10 ml) vinegar
1-1/2 tsp (6 g) baking soda

FOR CREAM CHEESE FROSTING

4/5 cup (225 g) cream cheese
4/5 cup plus 1 tbsp (225 g) mascarpone cheese
2 cups (225 g) icing sugar
1 tsp (5 ml) vanilla extract

PREPARATION

For red velvet cake: Preheat oven to 350°F (175°C).

Butter and flour two 9-inch cake pans. Set aside.

Using a hand or stand mixer, cream together butter and sugar. Add eggs one at a time and mix well. Pour in food coloring and vanilla and mix well, and then add flour and cocoa powder, alternating it with the buttermilk.

In another bowl, combine vinegar and baking soda and let sit for a few seconds. Add to batter and mix until smooth; don't overmix.

Divide batter between prepared pans. Bake for 30 to 35 minutes, or until a toothpick inserted into the center comes out clean. Let cake cool for about 5 minutes and then remove from pans. Let cool completely before icing.

For cream cheese frosting: Using a hand or stand mixer, mix together all icing ingredients, about 4 minutes or until icing is light and fluffy.

To assemble cake: Using a serrated knife, carefully cut off the slightly rounded top of each cake. Spread a thick, even layer of frosting over the top of one cake and place the other cake on top. Cover the top and sides with remaining frosting.

PORTUGUESE NATAS

9

MAKES 12 NATAS
PREP TIME: 1 HOUR

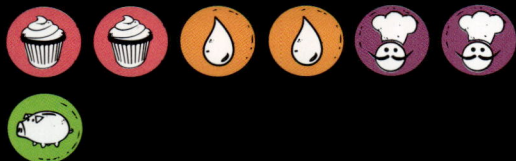

INGREDIENTS

1 package (about 1 lb) store-bought puff pastry
1/4 cup (32 g) flour
2 tbsp (20 g) cornstarch
1 cup (250 ml) milk
1/2 cup (125 ml) water
1 cup (210 g) sugar
Zest of 1/2 lemon
2 cinnamon sticks
4 egg yolks, beaten
Icing sugar
Ground cinnamon

PREPARATION

To make the tart shells, lightly butter a muffin pan. Lightly flour a flat work surface and roll out puff pastry dough to about 1/8-inch thick. Using a round cookie cutter slightly bigger than the muffin pan cups, cut puff pastry into rounds. Place rounds in prepared muffin cups and refrigerate.

Preheat oven to 400°F (200°C).

Mix together cornstarch and 1/2 cup (125 ml) milk.

In a pot, bring the rest of the milk to a boil. As soon as it begins to boil, add flour and cornstarch mixture. Using a whisk, mix well until it starts to boil again. Remove from heat and strain if there are still a few lumps.

In another pot, bring water, sugar, lemon zest, and cinnamon sticks to a boil. Let simmer for 3 minutes, remove lemon zest and cinnamon sticks, and then pour into milk and flour mixture. Using a whisk, mix well, and then let cool slightly. Whisk in egg yolks (mixture should be warm, but not hot, when adding yolks).

Fill each tart shell with a bit of custard. Bake for 20 minutes, or until pastry is crisp and golden brown. Sprinkle each nata with icing sugar or a bit of cinnamon.

TASTY TIP

If you don't have a cookie cutter, a cup, bowl, or empty can of the same size will work just as well.

DID YOU KNOW?

There's a good reason why you've probably seen these small custard tarts in the windows of Chinatown bakeries: *Pastéis de nata* were introduced to China by one of its Portuguese-occupied regions, and have become one of the country's most popular sweet treats.

CARROT CAKE WITH CREAM CHEESE ICING

SERVES 6
PREP TIME: 1 HOUR

DID YOU KNOW?

The modern orange carrot was developed in the Netherlands in the 17th century to honor William of Orange, by crossbreeding yellow and red varieties; prior to this, the most common carrot colors were purple, red, white, and yellow.

FOR CAKE

1 cup (150 g) flour
2 tsp (10 g) baking powder
1/4 tsp (1 g) salt
1/4 tsp (1 g) ground cinnamon
1/3 cup (80 g) unsalted butter, softened
1/2 cup (115 g) brown sugar, lightly packed
1/3 cup plus 1 tsp (75 g) sugar
Seeds from 1 vanilla bean
2 eggs
3 tbsp (45 ml) grapeseed oil
1-1/2 cups (175 g) carrots, grated with a microplane grater

FOR MAPLE MASCARPONE ICING

1-4/5 cups (475 g) mascarpone cheese
1/2 cup (125 ml) pure maple syrup

PREPARATION

For cake: Preheat oven to 350°F (175°C).

Sift flour, baking powder, salt, and cinnamon together into a bowl and set aside.

In another bowl, cream together butter, brown sugar, sugar, and vanilla bean seeds. Add eggs one at a time, mixing after each addition, and then add grapeseed oil.Mix well with a whisk. Add dry ingredients and mix with a wooden spoon until well incorporated. Stir in carrots, but don't overmix.

Pour batter into a buttered and floured 6-inch baking pan and bake for 35 minutes, or until a toothpick inserted into the center comes out clean.

For icing: In a bowl, and using a spatula, fold together mascarpone and maple syrup.

Serve each slice of cake with a generous spoonful of maple mascarpone icing, or ice the entire cake before serving.

HOLIDAY FRUITCAKE

SERVES 10
PREP TIME: 2 HOURS AND 15 MINUTES

REST TIME: 1 WEEK

FOR FRUITCAKE

1 cup (150 g) walnuts, roughly chopped
2-1/3 cups (300 g) pecans, roughly chopped
1-1/3 cups (440 g) dates, pitted and diced
1-1/3 cups (200 g) dried cranberries
1-1/3 cups (200 g) golden raisins
3/4 cup (135 g) pitted prunes, chopped
1/2 cup (50 g) candied orange peel
4 eggs
3/4 cup (150 g) sugar
2-1/3 cups (300 g) flour
1/8 tsp (1/2 g) salt

FOR SYRUP

1 cup (250 ml) water
1-1/2 cups (300 g) sugar
3/4 cup (180 ml) dark rum

PREPARATION

For syrup: In a pot, bring water and sugar to a boil. Remove from heat immediately, let cool to room temperature, and chill in the refrigerator. Stir in dark rum.

For fruitcake: Preheat oven to 350°F (175°C). Butter a 5-inch x 10-inch loaf pan and line bottom and sides with parchment paper.

In a bowl, combine nuts and dried and candied fruit.

In another bowl, beat together eggs and sugar.

Combine nuts and fruit with flour and salt. Mix well. Add egg and sugar mixture and mix well. Transfer to prepared loaf pan and press down firmly to compact. Cover with aluminum foil and bake for 45 minutes. After 45 minutes, remove foil, lower oven temperature to 325°F (160°C), and bake for 30 minutes longer, or until a toothpick inserted into the center comes out clean and the cake is lightly golden. Remove from pan immediately and let cool to room temperature.

Transfer to an airtight container and store in a cool place. Brush cake with syrup every day for a week. Slice and serve.

KING CAKE

SERVES 10
PREP TIME: 1 HOUR

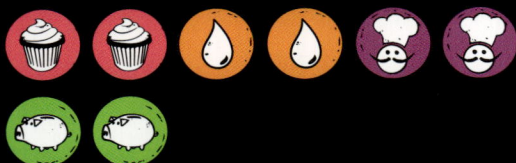

INGREDIENTS

1/3 cup plus 2 tbsp (100 g) unsalted butter, softened
1/2 cup (100 g) sugar
1 pinch salt
1 egg
1 cup (100 g) almond flour
1 tbsp (8 g) flour
1 tsp (5 ml) almond extract
1 package (about 1 lb) store-bought puff pastry
1 egg, beaten (for egg wash)

PREPARATION

Preheat oven to 400°F (200°C).

Using a hand or stand mixer, cream together butter, sugar, and salt. Add egg, and then add almond flour, flour, and vanilla extract. Chill in the refrigerator.

Divide puff pastry into two pieces. Lightly flour a flat work surface and roll out each piece into an 8-inch circle. Lightly sprinkle with flour, as needed, to prevent it from sticking. Transfer one of the circles to a baking sheet lined with parchment paper, or a silicone baking mat. Spread chilled mixture over top, leaving a 1-inch uncovered border. Moisten the uncovered border with a brush dipped in water, and then lay the second pastry circle over top. Press the edges well to seal.

With a fork or knife, cut a design into the top of the pastry. Brush with egg wash and then bake for 25 to 30 minutes.

DID YOU KNOW?

Traditionally, a small porcelain figurine is hidden in the cake, and the person who finds it becomes "king" or "queen" for a day! Often, bakeries will even give out a paper crown with each cake.

13

CREAMY HOT CHOCOLATE

SERVES 2
PREP TIME: 10 MINUTES

INGREDIENTS

3 cups (750 ml) milk
3/4 cup (140 g) dark or milk chocolate, roughly chopped

PREPARATION

In a pot, bring milk to a boil.

Remove pot from heat and add chocolate. Whisk until smooth and creamy. Pour into cups, top with whipped cream, and enjoy!

TASTY TIP

Adding a pinch of cardamom, cayenne, or cinnamon (or a bit of all three) will transport you to the warm beaches of Mexico on a cold winter night!

DID YOU KNOW?

The Mayas and Aztecs drank a beverage made from grilled, ground cocoa beans mixed with water, cornmeal, chili peppers, and spices like cinnamon and vanilla. This drink was actually quite bitter, and was consumed at sacred ceremonies and believed to be a health elixir.

14

THE LEMON MERINGUE PIE

SERVES 8
PREP TIME: 45 MINUTES

REST TIME: 3 HOURS

TASTY TIP

Don't worry if you don't have a kitchen torch—the broiler also does a fine job! Just make sure to keep a close eye on your pie, as meringue browns very quickly.

DID YOU KNOW?

Meringue can also be baked at a very low temperature into small, very crisp biscuits.

---

1 sweet pastry crust, prebaked (see recipe on page 027)

FOR LEMON FILLING

1/2 cup (120 g) unsalted butter
2/5 cup plus 4 tsp (120 ml) lemon juice
4 eggs
1 cup (200 g) sugar

FOR MERINGUE

3 egg whites
1-1/2 cups (190 g) icing sugar

PREPARATION

Preheat oven to 350°F (175°C).

For lemon filling: In a pot, melt butter with lemon juice over low heat. Meanwhile, whisk together eggs and sugar. As soon as butter is melted, add egg and sugar mixture. Cook over medium heat, whisking constantly. As soon as the mixture starts to bubble, remove from heat and pour into pie crust. Bake for 15 minutes. Let cool to room temperature and then chill in the refrigerator for at least 3 hours.

For meringue: In a bain-marie, heat egg yolks with icing sugar, whisking constantly, until the temperature reaches 120°F (50°C). Transfer to a bowl and, using a hand or stand mixer, whip at medium speed until stiff peaks form.

Top pie with meringue and, using a kitchen torch, lightly toast topping until golden brown. Serve.

15

CHIC CLAFOUTIS

SERVES 6
PREP TIME: 1 HOUR AND 40 MINUTES

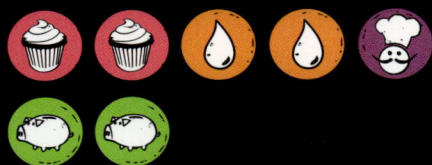

INGREDIENTS

3/4 cup (150 g) sugar
3 eggs
3/4 cup plus 2 tbsp (125 g) flour, sifted
3/4 cup (180 ml) 35% cream
2/5 cup (85 g) sour cream
1 tbsp (15 ml) kirsch
1-1/2 cups (250 g) black cherries, washed and pitted

PREPARATION

In a bowl, and using a whisk, combine sugar and eggs. Add flour. Add cream, sour cream, and kirsch. Refrigerate for 1 hour.

Preheat oven to 350°F (175°C). Pour batter into a buttered 10-inch baking dish and then top with cherries.

Bake for 25 to 30 minutes.

DID YOU KNOW?

Clafoutis comes from the Limousin region of France. Purists believe that a true clafoutis can only be made with cherries.

16

THE CRÈME BRÛLÉE

SERVES 8
PREP TIME: 1 HOUR AND 15 MINUTES

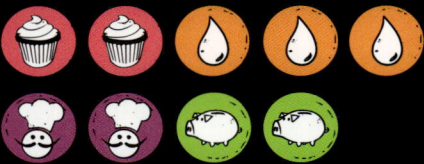

REST TIME: 3 HOURS

INGREDIENTS

2 cups (480 ml) 35% cream
2 cups (500 ml) milk
10 egg yolks
3/4 cup plus 2 tsp (160 g) sugar
Seeds from 1 vanilla bean
Sugar to caramelize

PREPARATION

Preheat oven to 280°F (140°C).

In a pot, bring cream and milk to a boil.

Meanwhile, in a bowl, whisk together egg yolks, sugar, and vanilla bean seeds.

As soon as the milk and cream mixture starts to bubble, remove from heat and slowly pour liquid into egg yolk mixture, whisking constantly. Pour into oven-safe ramekins and then place ramekins in a roasting pan or an oven-safe dish at least 2 inches deep. Pour water into roasting pan or dish, about halfway up ramekins.

Bake for 60 minutes. The crème brûlées should be firm but still slightly jiggly when gently shaken.

Leave in dish and let cool. Cover ramekins and chill in the refrigerator for at least 3 hours.

Right before serving, sprinkle the top of each crème brûlée with sugar and caramelize with a kitchen torch or under the broiler.

TASTY TIP

Add a hint of lemon, maple, or orange to your crème brulée... the possibilities are endless!

PUMPKIN CREAM CANNOLI

17

MAKES 25 CANNOLI
PREP TIME: 30 MINUTES

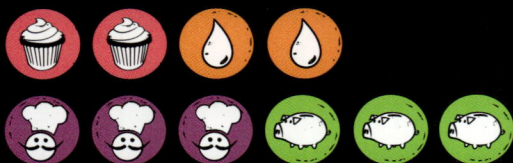

REST TIME: 2 HOURS

TASTY TIP

If you're in a rush, use store-bought waffle or sugar cones! If you're only missing the metal cannoli tubes, use cannelloni pasta tubes, which are sold at most grocery stores.

DID YOU KNOW?

In Francis Ford Coppola's celebrated film *The Godfather*, Clemenza's wife asks him to stop and pick up some cannoli on his way home, which he does—right before shooting another gangster. After the murder, Clemenza utters one of the most famous lines in the movie: "Leave the gun. Take the cannoli."

FOR CANNOLI SHELLS

1-3/4 cups (230 g) flour
3/4 cup (180 ml) red wine
1 tbsp (13 g) sugar
1 pinch salt
2 tbsp (30 ml) unsalted butter, melted
1 egg white

FOR PUMPKIN CREAM

1/2 cup plus 1 tsp (140 g) homemade pumpkin purée
(see recipe on page 046)
1 egg
3 tbsp (45 ml) 35% cream
8 tsp (35 g) brown sugar
1/4 tsp (1 g) ground cinnamon
1/8 tsp (1/2 g) ground ginger
1 pinch ground nutmeg
1/8 tsp (1/2 g) salt

FOR PUMPKIN RICOTTA FILLING

1 cup (250 g) 14% ricotta cheese, drained
4/5 cup plus 2 tbsp (240 g) pumpkin cream (see recipe above)
Zest of 1/2 orange
Seeds from 1/2 vanilla bean
1/2 cup plus 1 tbsp (140 ml) 35% cream, whipped

PREPARATION

For cannoli shells: Using a hand or stand mixer with the dough hook attachment, combine all ingredients, and mix for 5 minutes. Wrap dough with plastic wrap and chill for 2 hours.

In a fryer, heat vegetable oil to 350°F (175°C). Lightly flour a flat work surface and roll out dough until paper thin, sprinkling with flour as needed to prevent dough from sticking. Using a knife, cut dough into 3-inch squares. Roll squares around metal cannoli tubes and dab a bit of water where the ends overlap to seal the dough. Carefully place dough-wrapped tubes in the hot oil and fry until golden brown. Drain on paper towels.

For pumpkin cream: Prepare pumpkin purée, following the recipe on page 046. Combine with remaining pumpkin cream ingredients, transfer to a pan, and bake, again following the recipe on page 046. When mixture is cooked, strain with a fine wire mesh strainer to obtain a very smooth cream. Refrigerate.

For pumpkin ricotta filling: In a bowl, combine ricotta cheese, pumpkin cream, orange zest, and vanilla bean seeds. Using a spatula, fold in whipped cream. Transfer filling to a pastry bag with a large round tip and pipe into cannoli shells.

18

GRANDMA'S APPLE PIE

SERVES 8
PREP TIME: 1 HOUR AND 10 MINUTES

INGREDIENTS

8 large baking apples (McIntosh, Lobo, Honey Crisp, etc.), cored, peeled, and cut into 1-inch cubes
1/2 cup (115 g) brown sugar, lightly packed
1/4 tsp (1 g) cinnamon
2 tbsp (16 g) cornstarch
3 tbsp (43 g) unsalted butter, melted
2 portions basic pie pastry, the equivalent of 2 crusts
(see recipe on page 027)
1 egg, beaten with a bit of water (for egg wash)
Sugar

PREPARATION

Preheat oven to 375°F (190°C).

In a bowl, combine apples, brown sugar, cinnamon, cornstarch, and butter.

Roll out a portion of the pie crust dough and place in a 9-inch pie pan. Fill crust with apple mixture. Brush crust edges with egg wash and then place the second, rolled-out portion over top. Using a knife, trim off any excess dough around the edges. Cut a vent hole in the center of the crust, and pinch around the edges to seal.

Brush top crust with egg wash and sprinkle with sugar. Bake for 35 to 40 minutes.

TASTY TIP

For homestyle lattice-top apple pie, cut the dough into even strips. Lay out half of the strips of dough in parallel lines over the apple pie filling. Weave the remaining strips in the other direction, under and then over the first set of strips.

19

TRUFFLES THREE WAYS

MAKES 40 TRUFFLES
PREP TIME: 4 HOURS

TASTY TIP

Roll your truffles in:

- Cocoa powder
- Finely chopped, toasted nuts
- Coconut

These are just a few simple suggestions. Experiment with different ingredients like dried lavender, crushed cookies, and spices, and create YOUR very best truffles!

DID YOU KNOW?

Elegant, decadent chocolate truffles take their name from real truffles, the highly prized fungus they so closely resemble.

3/4 cup (100 g) dark or milk chocolate, for garnish

FOR RUM TRUFFLES

1 cup (250 ml) 35% cream
2 cups (275 g) dark chocolate, chopped
3 tbsp (45 g) unsalted butter, softened
3 tbsp (45 ml) rum

FOR ORANGE TRUFFLES

1 cup (250 ml) 35% cream
2 cups (275 g) dark chocolate, chopped
3 tsp (45 g) unsalted butter, softened
Zest of 1 orange
3 tbsp (45 ml) orange liqueur

FOR TEA TRUFFLES

1/3 cup (80 ml) 35% cream
1/3 cup (80 ml) milk
1/2 tbsp (7 g) Earl Grey tea
3/4 cup (138 g) dark chocolate, chopped
3/4 cup (138 g) milk chocolate, chopped
2 tbsp (30 g) unsalted butter, softened

PREPARATION

For rum truffles: In a pot, bring cream to a boil and remove immediately from heat. Using a spatula, fold in chocolate and butter. Add rum, cover, and chill until firm enough to shape into truffles.

For orange truffles: In a pot, bring cream to a boil and remove immediately from heat. Using a spatula, fold in chocolate, butter, and orange zest. Add orange liqueur, cover, and chill until firm enough to shape into truffles.

For tea truffles: In a pot, bring cream to a boil and remove immediately from heat. Add tea, cover, and allow to infuse for 10 minutes. Strain using a wire mesh sieve. In the same pot, bring the cream and tea infusion back up to a boil and remove immediately from heat. Using a spatula, fold in chocolate and butter. Chill until firm enough to shape into truffles.

Using a spoon, shape mixture into small balls and then refrigerate for 30 minutes. Put a bit of melted chocolate in the palm of one hand and, using the other palm, roll each truffle in the chocolate to completely coat, adding more chocolate as needed. Roll in coating of your choice, if desired. Store truffles in the refrigerator.

20

TROPICAL DELIGHT

SERVES 8
PREP TIME: 1 HOUR

INGREDIENTS

1 fresh, ripe pineapple
1 cup (250 ml) orange juice
1 ripe banana
1 cup (200 g) sugar
1/3 cup (80 ml) water
1 vanilla bean, halved, seeds scraped out and reserved
3 tbsp (30 g) fresh ginger, peeled and finely chopped
Juice and zest of 1 lime

PREPARATION

Preheat oven to 350°F (175°C).

Peel pineapple and remove "eyes" with a knife. Cut into 4 long pieces and remove core. Place in a roasting pan and set aside.

With a hand blender, combine orange juice and banana. Set aside.

In a pot, bring sugar and water to a boil and cook until the mixture turns a medium golden color. Remove from heat. Pour in orange juice and banana mixture in a slow, steady stream. Be very careful during this step, as the hot mixture may splatter. Add vanilla bean pod and seeds, ginger, and lime juice and zest. Bring back up to a boil and pour over pineapple.

Bake for 30 minutes, or until pineapple is tender, turning occasionally. Serve hot.

21

TRIPLE CHOCOLATE COOKIES

MAKES 16 COOKIES
PREP TIME: 30 MINUTES

INGREDIENTS

1 cup (145 g) flour
1/2 tsp (2-1/2 g) baking powder
3 tbsp (20 g) cocoa powder
1/2 cup (125 g) unsalted butter, softened
1 cup (220 g) brown sugar, lightly packed
1 tsp (4 g) salt
1 egg
1-3/4 cups (240 g) dark chocolate, roughly chopped
3/4 cup (115 g) milk chocolate, roughly chopped

PREPARATION

Preheat oven to 350°F (175°C).

In a bowl, combine flour, baking powder, and cocoa powder. Set aside.

In another bowl, cream together butter, brown sugar, and salt. Add egg. Add dry ingredients, and then stir in chocolate.

Using spoons, shape dough into small balls (about 2 tbsp each) and drop onto a baking sheet lined with parchment paper, or a silicone baking mat.

Bake for 10 minutes. Cookies should be soft in the center.

22

FROZEN POP TRIO

MAKES 10 POPS
PREP TIME: 15 MINUTES

FREEZING TIME: 5 HOURS AND 45 MINUTES

FOR MIMOSA POPS

2/3 cup (160 ml) water
3/4 cup (150 g) sugar
1-3/5 cups (400 ml) orange juice
1-3/5 cups plus 2 tbsp sparkling wine

FOR MANGO LASSI POPS

2 mangoes, peeled and diced
1 cup (250 ml) plain yogurt
1 cup (250 ml) milk
3 tbsp (45 ml) honey

FOR WATERMELON POPS

6 cups (965 g) watermelon, seeded and diced
1/3 cup (70 g) sugar

PREPARATION

For mimosa pops: In a pot, bring water and sugar to a boil. Let simmer for 3 minutes. Mix together with orange juice and sparkling wine. Pour into popsicle molds, insert popsicle sticks, and freeze.

For mango lassi pops: Using a hand blender, purée mangoes, yogurt, milk, and honey until smooth. Pour into popsicle molds, insert popsicle sticks, and freeze.

For watermelon pops: Using a hand blender, purée watermelon and sugar together. Pour into popsicle molds, insert popsicle sticks, and freeze.

23

SWEET PEAR & ALMOND TART

SERVES 6
PREP TIME: 1 HOUR

1 sweet pastry crust, prebaked (see recipe on page 027)

FOR POACHED PEARS

4 cups water
Juice and zest of 1 lemon
2 star anise
10 whole peppercorns, crushed
1 vanilla bean
1 cup (200 g) sugar
4 ripe pears, peeled

FOR ALMOND FILLING

1/2 cup (115 g) unsalted butter, softened
Seeds from 1 vanilla bean
1/2 cup plus 2 tbsp (120 g) sugar
1-1/2 cups (150 g) almond flour
3 eggs
1 tsp (5 ml) almond extract
1/3 cup (50 g) flour

PREPARATION

For poached pears: In a pot, whisk together all ingredients, except pears, until sugar is completely dissolved. Place pears in the liquid and bring to a boil. As soon as the liquid begins to boil, reduce heat to low. Cover pears with a circle of parchment paper and cook for 15 to 20 minutes, or until pears are tender (test with the tip of a knife). Remove from heat and let cool completely in the syrup.

For almond filling: In a bowl, cream together butter, vanilla bean seeds, and sugar. Add almond flour. Add eggs one at a time, mixing after each addition. Finish by stirring in almond extract and flour. Refrigerate.

Preheat oven to 350°F (175°C).

Spread almond filling evenly in baked crust. Cut pears in half lengthwise and remove cores using a small spoon. Very thinly slice pears and place over almond filling.

Bake for 20 minutes, or until tart is golden brown.

TASTY TIP

In a pinch, use drained canned peaches. It will save you time and still taste absolutely marvelous!

NOUGAT ICE CREAM

24

SERVES 8
PREP TIME: 1 HOUR

FREEZING TIME: 6 HOURS

DID YOU KNOW?

The Romans believed that almonds were a symbol of fertility. Wedding guests would shower newly married couples with the sweet nut in the hopes that it would bring them good fortune.

FOR CARAMELIZED NUTS

3-1/2 tbsp (44 g) sugar
2 tbsp (30 ml) water
3/4 cup (104 g) pistachios and almonds

FOR NOUGAT

2 tbsp (30 ml) honey
1-1/2 cups (375 ml) 35% cream
3 egg whites
1/2 cup (105 g) sugar
3/4 cup (104 g) caramelized nuts, roughly chopped
(see recipe above)
3/4 cup (130 g) candied orange

PREPARATION

For caramelized nuts: In a pot, bring sugar and water to a boil. Cook over medium-high heat until mixture turns a medium golden brown color. Remove from heat and add nuts. Stir with a wooden spoon to coat.

Spread onto a baking sheet lined with parchment paper, or a silicone baking mat. Let cool completely, roughly chop, and set aside.

For nougat: In the microwave, heat honey with 1 tbsp (15 ml) 35% cream. Set aside.

Using a hand or stand mixer with the whisk attachment, whip remaining cream until stiff peaks form. Carefully fold in hot honey and cream mixture with a flexible plastic spatula. Refrigerate.

Using a hand or stand mixer with the whisk attachment, beat egg whites until stiff peaks form, gradually sprinkling in sugar.

Fold egg whites, along with nut mixture and candied orange, into cream and honey mixture. Pour into a buttered square or loaf pan and top with a piece of parchment paper. Freeze for at least 6 hours.

Slice and serve.

25

CHOCO-CHERRY-CARAMEL CUPS

SERVES 6
PREP TIME: 2 HOURS

FREEZING TIME: 7 HOURS

INGREDIENTS

1 brownie, cut into 1-inch cubes (see recipe on page 032)
1-1/2 cups (250 g) cherries, washed, pitted, and halved

FOR DARK BEER ICE CREAM

1 cup plus 2 tbsp (280 ml) dark beer
1/4 cup (60 ml) molasses
2 cups (500 ml) milk
2 cups (500 ml) 35% cream
1/2 cup plus 1 tbsp (120 g) sugar
8 egg yolks

FOR CARAMEL

5 tbsp (75 ml) 35% cream
2 tbsp (30 ml) water
1/2 cup plus 2 tbsp (120 g) sugar
1 tbsp (15 ml) clear corn syrup
1/8 tsp (1/2 g) sea salt
2 tbsp (28 g) unsalted butter

PREPARATION

For dark beer ice cream: In a pot, bring beer and molasses to a boil. Remove from heat and set aside.

In a pot, bring milk, cream, and half of the sugar to a boil. Set aside.

In a bowl, combine egg yolks and remaining sugar, whisking vigorously. Pour a bit of the milk, cream, and sugar mixture into the egg yolk mixture, whisking constantly, and then pour back into the pot with the remaining milk and cream mixture. Cook on the stovetop, stirring constantly with a wooden spoon, until the temperature reaches 180°F (82°C). Remove from heat and strain with a fine wire mesh strainer. Stir in dark beer mixture and refrigerate until completely cool. Transfer to an ice cream maker and freeze according to manufacturer's directions.

For caramel: In a pot, heat cream. Set aside. In another pot, bring water, sugar, corn syrup, and sea salt to a boil. Cook, without stirring, until the mixture turns a medium golden brown. Pour in the hot cream in a slow, steady stream, whisking gently and constantly. Be very careful during this step, as the hot mixture may splatter. Add butter and chill. Refrigerate until ready to serve.

For brownie "croutons," preheat oven to 350°F (175°C). Place brownie cubes on a baking sheet and cook for 10 minutes, stirring occasionally, to allow them to dry out slightly.

Place brownies and cherries in a large serving bowl, or in small individual bowls, and top with hot caramel and ice cream.

26

BLUEBERRY CASHEW CHEESECAKE

SERVES 12
PREP TIME: 1 HOUR AND 30 MINUTES

REST TIME: 4 HOURS

TASTY TIP

If you can't find cashew butter, use unsweetened, all-natural peanut butter instead.

FOR GRAHAM CRACKER CRUST

1 cup (90 g) graham cracker crumbs
1/3 cup (45 g) pecans, chopped
2 tbsp (30 g) sugar
1/3 cup (80 ml) unsalted butter, melted

FOR CHEESECAKE FILLING

3 packages (8 oz each) cream cheese,
brought to room temperature
1 cup plus 2 tbsp (230 g) sugar
Seeds from 1 vanilla bean
1 cup (250 g) cashew butter
4 eggs
1/4 cup plus 2 tsp (75 g) sour cream
1/4 cup (60 ml) 35% cream
2/5 cup plus 2 tbsp (60 g) cashews, roughly chopped

FOR BLUEBERRY TOPPING

1/4 cup (60 ml) honey
1/4 cup (60 ml) water
3 cups (460 g) fresh or frozen blueberries

PREPARATION

Preheat oven to 350°F (175°C).

For graham cracker crust: In a bowl, combine graham cracker crumbs, chopped pecans, sugar, and melted butter. Press mixture firmly into the bottom of an 8-inch springform pan. Bake for 8 minutes and then let cool to room temperature.

For cheesecake filling: Using a hand or stand mixer with the whisk attachment, beat cream cheese together with sugar, vanilla bean seeds, and cashew butter. Add eggs one at a time, mixing after each addition, and then add sour cream and 35% cream.

Pour into springform pan and sprinkle cashews over top. Wrap bottom and sides of pan with a large piece of aluminum foil and set in a large roasting pan or baking dish. Pour enough water into the roasting pan to come halfway up the sides of the springform pan. Bake for 1 hour and then let cool completely in the roasting pan. Chill in the refrigerator for at least 3 hours.

For blueberry topping: In a pot, bring honey and water to a boil. As soon as it starts to bubble, add blueberries and cook for 5 minutes. Transfer to a bowl and let cool before spooning over top of cheesecake. Serve.

27

STICKY TOFFEE PUDDING

SERVES 8
PREP TIME: 1 HOUR

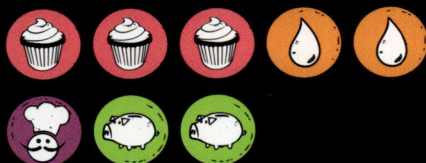

FOR PUDDING

1-1/5 cups (225 g) dates, pitted
2 ripe bananas
6 tbsp (85 g) unsalted butter, softened
4/5 cup (170 g) sugar
2 eggs
1-1/4 cups plus 2 tbsp (170 g) flour, sifted
2 tsp (10 g) baking powder
1/4 tsp (1 g) cinnamon
1/4 tsp (1 g) ground nutmeg
1/2 cup plus 1 tsp (100 g) dates, pitted and diced

FOR TOFFEE SAUCE

1-3/4 cups (400 g) brown sugar, lightly packed
1/2 cup (125 g) unsalted butter
2 cups (500 ml) 35% cream

PREPARATION

For pudding: Preheat oven to 375°F (190°C) and butter 8 ramekins.

Soak 1-1/5 cups dates in boiling water. When dates are soft, drain and purée in a food processor with bananas, until smooth. Set aside.

In a bowl, whisk together butter and sugar. Add eggs one at a time, mixing after each addition. Add flour, baking powder, and ground spices. Finish by stirring in date and banana purée, and diced dates. Transfer batter to the ramekins and bake for 25 minutes, or until a toothpick inserted into the center comes out clean.

For toffee sauce: In a pot, combine all ingredients and bring to a boil. Let simmer for 5 minutes.

Serve hot with a generous ladleful of toffee sauce.

TASTY TIP

Top with toasted nuts or a scoop of vanilla ice cream... or why not both?

28

BAKLAVA

MAKES 15 SQUARES
PREP TIME: 1 HOUR AND 15 MINUTES

REST TIME: 5 HOURS

DID YOU KNOW?

Traditional Greek baklava is supposed to have 33 layers, one for each year of Jesus's life.

FOR SYRUP

1 cup (250 ml) water
1 cup (250 ml) honey
1 cup (210 g) sugar
1 cinnamon stick
Zest of 1 orange

FOR BAKLAVA

1-1/5 cups (180 g) whole blanched almonds
1-1/3 cups (180 g) whole pistachios
2-1/4 cups (240 g) walnuts
12 sheets phyllo pastry, cut into 8-inch x 12-inch rectangles
1/2 cup (125 g) unsalted butter, melted

PREPARATION

For syrup: In a pot, bring all syrup ingredients to a boil. Refrigerate.

For filling: In a food processor, finely chop nuts. Set aside.

Preheat oven to 375°F (190°C). Brush 3 phyllo sheets with melted butter and carefully place at the bottom of an 8-inch x 12-inch baking pan. Spread 1/3 of the nut mixture evenly over top. Repeat this process two more times and finish with a layer of 3 buttered phyllo sheets.

Bake for 30 minutes, or until phyllo is golden brown. As soon as the baklava comes out of the oven, pour the syrup evenly over top. Let sit at room temperature for 5 hours. Serve.

29

CHURROS

MAKES 18 CHURROS
PREP TIME: 1 HOUR AND 50 MINUTES

TASTY TIP

If you're not a fan of caramel, melt chocolate or hazelnut spread and use it for dipping.

DID YOU KNOW?

In Argentina and Peru, churros are filled with *dulce de leche*.

FOR DULCE DE LECHE

1 can (10 oz) sweetened condensed milk

FOR CHURROS

1 cup (250 ml) milk
1/2 cup (125 g) unsalted butter
1 pinch salt
1 pinch sugar
1-1/2 cups (220 g) flour, sifted
3 eggs
Vegetable oil for frying
Sugar

PREPARATION

For dulce de leche: Remove paper label from can, but don't open it. Place can in a pot and cover with water. Cover and let simmer for 1 hour and 30 minutes. Let can cool slightly before opening. Dip churros into dulce de leche and enjoy!

For churros: In a pot, bring milk, butter, salt, and sugar to a boil. Remove from heat and add flour all at once; mix well with a wooden spoon.

Add eggs one at a time, mixing well after each addition. Transfer dough to a pastry bag with a large open-star tip and refrigerate for 30 minutes. When dough is chilled, pipe directly into the oil that has been preheated to 320-340°F (160-170°C). Fry until golden brown, drain on paper towels, and roll in sugar.

30

PECAN & BOURBON PIE

SERVES 10
PREP TIME: 1 HOUR

INGREDIENTS

3/4 cup (180 ml) corn syrup
3 tbsp (40 g) sugar
1/4 cup (50 g) brown sugar, lightly packed
3 tbsp (45 g) unsalted butter, melted
1/8 tsp (1/2 g) salt
Seeds from 1/2 vanilla bean
2-1/2 tbsp (38 ml) bourbon
3 eggs, beaten
2 cups (195 g) whole pecans
1 sweet pastry crust, prebaked (see recipe on page 027)

PREPARATION

Preheat oven to 350°F (175°C).

In a bowl, combine corn syrup, sugar, brown sugar, butter, salt, vanilla bean seeds, and bourbon. Stir in eggs and half of the pecans, and then spread mixture evenly in the pie crust. Arrange remaining pecans over top. Bake for 35 to 40 minutes. Pie filling should still be jiggly in the center when gently shaken. Let cool to room temperature and serve.

31

DOUBLE FRUIT CRISP

SERVES 6
PREP TIME: 40 MINUTES

FOR CRISP TOPPING

1/2 cup (75 g) flour
3 tbsp (40 g) brown sugar
3 tbsp (42 g) unsalted butter
1 cup (85 g) rolled (old-fashioned) oats
1 cup (105 g) pecans, roughly chopped
1/4 tsp (1 g) cinnamon

FOR FILLING

1-1/2 cups (230 g) wild blueberries
3 ripe peaches, peeled, pitted and diced
1/4 cup (57 g) brown sugar, lightly packed
Zest of 1/2 lemon

PREPARATION

Preheat oven to 350°F (175°C).

Combine all crisp topping ingredients, mixing until texture is crumbly and clumps form. Set aside.

In a bowl, combine blueberries, peaches, brown sugar, and lemon zest. Transfer to an 8-inch square baking dish. Sprinkle topping evenly over top.

Bake for 20 minutes, until topping is golden brown. Serve.

32

DOUGHNUTS

MAKES 15 DOUGHNUTS
PREP TIME: 1 HOUR AND 20 MINUTES

TASTY TIP

If you don't have a stand mixer, squeeze in an extra arm workout by kneading the dough by hand!

Make powdered doughnuts by replacing the cinnamon with icing sugar. Just don't forget to lick your fingers after!

DID YOU KNOW?

The origin of the ring-shaped doughnut is heavily debated, but one story claims that an American, Hanson Gregory, invented it in 1847 when he was just 16! Gregory worked on a ship, where fried batter was typical fare; however, he found the greasy edges and uncooked center to be unappetizing. His solution was to use the ship's round tin pepper box to punch a hole in the dough to get rid of the raw middle and allow the doughnut to cook evenly.

FOR DOUGHNUT DOUGH

2 cups (300 g) flour
1/4 cup (52 g) sugar
1 tbsp (15 g) fresh active yeast
(also called compressed or cake yeast)
1 egg
3 tbsp (45 ml) milk
6 tbsp (90 ml) water
2 tbsp (30 ml) butter, melted

INGREDIENTS

Vegetable oil for frying
1 cup (210 g) sugar
1 tsp (5 g) ground cinnamon

PREPARATION

Using a stand mixer with the dough hook attachment, combine all doughnut dough ingredients on medium speed. Let mixer knead dough, about 8 minutes, or until dough is smooth. Remove dough from hook, form into a ball, and transfer to a lightly floured bowl. Cover dough and let rise in a warm place until doubled in size, about 1 hour.

In a fryer, preheat oil to 350°F (175°C).

Place dough on a lightly floured, flat work surface. Using a rolling pin, roll out dough to about 1/2 inch thick, sprinkling on more flour as needed to prevent dough from sticking. Using a round cookie cutter, cut out donut circles and, using a smaller cookie cutter, cut out doughnut holes.

In a large bowl, combine sugar and cinnamon.

Carefully place doughnuts in oil, and cook on both sides until golden brown. Remove with a slotted spoon and drain on paper towels. Dip each doughnut in cinnamon sugar and enjoy!

33

FRESH FRUIT TARTS

SERVES 6
PREP TIME: 2 HOURS AND 5 MINUTES

1 portion sweet pastry, divided into 3 tart molds and prebaked (see recipe on page 027)

FOR PASTRY CREAM

2 cups (500 ml) milk
4/5 cup plus 7 tsp (200 g) sugar
4 tbsp (33 g) cornstarch
2 eggs
1/5 cup (50 g) unsalted butter, at room temperature
Fresh fruit of your choice (strawberries, raspberries, peaches, kiwis, etc.)

PREPARATION

For pastry cream: In a pot, bring 1-3/4 cups milk to a boil with half of the sugar.

Meanwhile, in a bowl, whisk together remaining sugar, remaining milk, cornstarch, and eggs.

As soon as the milk and sugar mixture starts to bubble, remove from heat and pour 1/3 into the egg mixture, whisking constantly. Mix well and pour into the pot with the rest of the milk and sugar mixture.

Bring back up to a boil and boil for 30 seconds, whisking constantly. After 30 seconds, remove from heat and add butter. Transfer to a bowl, cover immediately with plastic wrap, and refrigerate until completely cool.

Using a hand or stand mixer, whip pastry cream at high speed, mixing in the room temperature butter 1 tbsp at a time. Whip until creamy and stiff peaks form.

Spread pastry cream in the bottom of tart shells and top with fresh fruit of your choice.

34

THE TIRAMISU

SERVES 6
PREP TIME: 45 MINUTES

INGREDIENTS

3 eggs
1/3 cup (65 g) sugar
Seeds from 1 vanilla bean
2 cups (475 g) mascarpone cheese, brought to room temperature
1 cup (250 ml) espresso or strong coffee
24 ladyfinger cookies
Cocoa (for garnish)

PREPARATION

Using a hand or stand mixer, beat together eggs, sugar, and vanilla bean seeds for 5 minutes.

Add mascarpone cheese and beat for 2 to 3 minutes longer, until mixture is completely smooth.

Pour coffee into a bowl. Soak a few cookies at a time in the coffee and arrange at the bottom of a serving dish. Evenly spread a layer of mascarpone cream over soaked cookies and sprinkle with cocoa. Continue layering until you run out of ingredients and then finish with a dusting of cocoa. Refrigerate until ready to serve.

TASTY TIP

Add 1 oz of the liqueur or alcohol of your choice (Tia Maria, Marsala, rum, etc.) to the coffee.

Serve tiramisu in individual glasses or ramekins, or make it a family-style dessert by layering the ingredients in a large dish. Because it doesn't need to be cooked, you can present it whichever way you prefer!

35

SUGAR PIE

SERVES 8
PREP TIME: 30 MINUTES

REST TIME: 2 HOURS

TASTY TIP

Prevent brown sugar from hardening by storing it in a tightly sealed container with a slice of bread or apple, or with a clay disc that can be bought at kitchen specialty stores.

INGREDIENTS

1 portion basic pie pastry (see recipe on page 027)
4 cups (725 g) brown sugar, unpacked
1 can (14 oz) unsweetened condensed milk
1 egg
1 tsp (5 ml) vanilla extract
2 tbsp (30 ml) corn syrup
1 tbsp (8 g) flour

PREPARATION

Preheat oven to 350°F (175°C).

Roll out pastry and transfer to a 9-inch pie pan.

Using a hand or stand mixer, combine all pie filling ingredients until the surface becomes frothy. Pour into pie crust.

Bake for 25 minutes. Let cool and refrigerate.

36

SCONES & JAM

MAKES 16 SCONES
PREP TIME: 1 HOUR AND 30 MINUTES

REST TIME: 30 MINUTES

TASTY TIP

Replace the raisins with any other dried fruit of your choice: figs, cranberries, candied orange, etc.

DID YOU KNOW?

The first scones were round and flat, about as big as a medium-size plate, and made with unleavened oats. The round cake, called bannock by the Scottish, was cooked in the oven on a griddle and then sliced into triangles for serving.

FOR SCONES

1 cup (153 g) golden raisins
5 cups plus 2 tbsp (675 g) flour
2 tbsp (23 g) baking powder
1/2 cup (100 g) sugar
Zest of 1 lemon
1 tsp (5 g) salt
1 cup (230 g) cold unsalted butter, cut into small cubes
1-1/2 cups (375 g) buttermilk
Milk
Sugar

FOR FIG JAM

3 cups (500 g) fresh figs, washed and cut into 1-inch pieces
1 cup plus 3 tbsp (250 g) sugar
1 tbsp (15 ml) lemon juice
1/3 cup (80 ml) water

PREPARATION

For scones: Soak raisins for 5 minutes in hot water to soften them. Drain well and set aside.

In a bowl, combine flour, baking powder, lemon zest, and salt. Add butter and, using your hands, mix dough until it has the texture of coarse crumbs. Add buttermilk and raisins and mix until just combined; don't overmix.

Transfer dough to a lightly floured, flat work surface and flatten into a 4-inch x 16-inch rectangle. Using a sharp knife, cut rectangle into 16 triangles. Transfer to a baking sheet lined with parchment paper, or a silicone baking mat, and chill for 30 minutes.

Preheat oven to 350°F (175°C).

Brush the top of each scone with a bit of milk, and sprinkle with sugar. Bake for 20 minutes.

For fig jam: In a pot, combine figs, sugar, lemon juice, and water. Cook over low heat, stirring often, for 1 hour, or until jam is thick enough to coat the back of a spoon. Let cool to room temperature, pour into an airtight container, and refrigerate.

Serve scones with fig jam and crème fraîche.

37

STRAWBERRIES & CHAMPAGNE

SERVES 6
PREP TIME: 20 MINUTES

REST TIME: 1 HOUR

INGREDIENTS

2-1/2 cups (450 g) strawberries, washed, hulled, and halved
Zest of 1 lemon
1 cup (250 ml) champagne, cava or sparkling wine
8 basil leaves, very thinly sliced
2 tbsp (26 g) sugar

PREPARATION

In a bowl, combine all ingredients. Chill for 1 hour in the refrigerator. Serve in champagne glasses.

38

CHOCOLATE LAVA CAKES

SERVES 8
PREP TIME: 45 MINUTES

INGREDIENTS

1-3/4 cups (240 g) dark chocolate, roughly chopped
1 cup plus 1 tbsp (240 g) unsalted butter
4 eggs
4 egg yolks
6 tbsp (75 g) sugar
2/3 cup (100 g) flour, sifted

PREPARATION

Preheat oven to 350°F (175°C).

Melt chocolate and butter in a bain-marie.

Using a hand or stand mixer, beat together eggs, egg yolks, and sugar for about 5 minutes.

When chocolate and butter are completely melted, carefully fold in egg mixture, and then gently stir in flour.

Butter and flour 8 ramekins (about 3-1/2 inches in diameter). Pour batter into each ramekin, about 2 inches up the sides. Bake for 15 minutes; centers should still be quite soft. Serve hot with your favorite ice cream.

TASTY TIP

If you're preparing your lava cakes ahead of time, shorten the baking time by 5 minutes. Let the cakes completely cool before flipping them out of the ramekins, and then reheat for 5 minutes before serving.

39

THE PARIS-BREST

SERVES 8
PREP TIME: 3 HOURS

TASTY TIP

Prepare the Paris-Brest "crown" in advance; just bake it, wrap it securely, and freeze it for up to one month.

DID YOU KNOW?

Paris-Brest was invented in 1910 to commemorate the bicycle race that takes place between the two French cities. Its shape, of course, is meant to represent a wheel.

FOR CHOUX PASTRY

1 cup (250 ml) milk
1/2 tbsp (7 g) sugar
1/2 tsp (2-1/2 g) salt
1/2 cup (115 g) unsalted butter
1 cup (150 g) flour
4 eggs
1 egg, beaten (for egg wash)
Sliced almonds
Icing sugar

FOR HAZELNUT PASTRY CREAM

1 recipe pastry cream (see recipe on page 108)
1/4 cup (60 ml) hazelnut praline spread

PREPARATION

Preheat oven to 350°F (175°C).

For hazelnut pastry cream: Follow pastry cream instructions on page 108. At the end, delicately whisk in hazelnut praline paste.

For choux pastry: In a pot, bring milk, sugar, salt, and butter to a boil over high heat. Remove from heat and add flour all at once. Mix well with a wooden spoon. Return to heat and, stirring constantly, cook for about 1 minute, until dough starts to pull away from the sides of the pan. Remove from heat and add eggs one at a time, stirring vigorously after each addition until dough is smooth. Transfer pastry to a pastry bag fitted with a 1/2-inch star tip.

On a piece of parchment paper, use a pencil to draw a 7-inch circle. Use this circle as a guide to make the Paris-Brest. Pipe a circle of dough onto the parchment paper. Pipe a second circle inside the first, ensuring the edges of both circles are always touching. Pipe a third circle over top of the first two to cover the seam. Brush with egg wash and sprinkle with almonds. Bake for 30 to 35 minutes, until pastry is lightly golden.

Cut pastry in half horizontally. Transfer pastry cream to a pastry bag fitted with a star tip and pipe onto the bottom half. Top with the other half of pastry and refrigerate. Sprinkle with icing sugar right before serving.

40

OLD-FASHIONED STRAWBERRY SHORTCAKE

SERVES 6
PREP TIME: 50 MINUTES

REST TIME: 1H00

FOR PASTRY

1-1/2 cups (220 g) flour
3-1/2 tbsp (45 g) sugar
3-1/2 tsp (13 g) baking powder
1/8 tsp (1/2 g) salt
2 tsp (10 g) lemon zest
6 tbsp (86 g) cold unsalted butter, cut into cubes
2 egg yolks
2/3 cup (160 ml) 35% cream

FOR TOPPING

1 cup (250 ml) 35% cream
1/5 cup (25 g) icing sugar
24 fresh strawberries, hulled and halved

PREPARATION

For pastry: In a bowl, combine flour, sugar, baking powder, salt, and lemon zest. Add butter and, using your hands, mix dough until it has the texture of coarse crumbs. In another bowl, and using a whisk, combine egg yolks and cream. Add to butter and dry ingredient mixture and mix until it becomes a dough. Wrap dough and chill in the refrigerator for 1 hour.

Preheat oven to 350°F (175°C).

Lightly flour a flat work surface and roll out dough to about 1 inch thick. Using a knife, cut dough into 3-inch squares. Transfer to a baking sheet lined with parchment paper, or a silicone baking mat. Bake for 20 minutes, or until scones are lightly golden. Let cool completely.

For topping: Whip together cream and icing sugar until stiff peaks form.

Slice each scone lengthwise. Top half of each scone with whipped cream and strawberries, close, and serve.

TASTY TIP

Use different fruit, depending on the season! These biscuits pair perfectly with other berries, as well as with stone fruit, like peaches and apricots.

41

KEY LIME PIE

SERVES 8
PREP TIME: 1 HOUR AND 15 MINUTES

FOR GRAHAM CRACKER CRUST

1-1/2 cups (133 g) graham cracker crumbs
1/4 cup (50 g) sugar
1/2 cup (115 g) unsalted butter, melted

FOR KEY LIME FILLING

4 egg yolks
1 can (14 oz) sweetened condensed milk
3/5 cup (150 ml) lime juice
1 tsp (5 g) lime zest
Whipped cream

PREPARATION

Preheat oven to 350°F (175°C).

For graham cracker crust: In a bowl, combine all graham cracker crust ingredients and press firmly into the bottom and up the sides of a 9-inch pie pan. Bake for 5 minutes.

For key lime filling: Whisk together egg yolks and sweetened condensed milk. Add lime juice and zest. Pour into prepared crust and bake for 15 minutes. Let cool and then refrigerate.

Right before serving, top each slice with a generous dollop of whipped cream.

DID YOU KNOW?

Lime was used by British sailors to prevent scurvy, a potentially fatal disease caused by vitamin C deficiency. This is how the British came to be known as "limeys"!

42

FRENCH MILLE-FEUILLES

SERVES 6
PREP TIME: 30 MINUTES

REST TIME: 3 HOURS

INGREDIENTS

2 cups (480 ml) 35% cream
1 cup (150 g) milk chocolate, roughly chopped
1 package (about 1 lb) store-bought puff pastry
2 cups (260 g) fresh raspberries
Icing sugar
Dark chocolate shavings

PREPARATION

For chocolate chantilly cream: In a pot, bring cream to a boil and remove from heat immediately. In a bowl, pour hot cream over chocolate and whisk until smooth. Let cool to room temperature, cover with plastic wrap, and refrigerate for at least 3 hours.

Preheat oven to 400°F (200°C).

To prepare the pastry, lightly flour a flat work surface and roll out dough until very thin. Transfer dough to a baking sheet lined with parchment paper and pierce with a fork all over. Refrigerate for 15 minutes and then bake for 25 to 30 minutes, or until pastry is golden brown and crisp. Let cool to room temperature. Using a serrated knife, cut into 2-inch x 4-inch rectangles.

Using a hand or stand mixer, whip chocolate cream until stiff peaks form. Chill in the refrigerator. Transfer chantilly cream to a pastry bag with a large round tip and pipe cream over one pastry rectangle. Lay another pastry rectangle on top of chantilly cream. Pipe more chantilly over the second rectangle and then top with a final piece of pastry. Pipe a bit more cream on top and then garnish with raspberries, icing sugar, and chocolate shavings. Repeat entire process with remaining ingredients and serve.

DID YOU KNOW?

If Chantilly cream is whipped for too long, it turns into butter!

43

FRENCH CANADIAN "PUDDING CHÔMEUR"

MAKES 10 SERVINGS
PREP TIME: 1 HOUR

TASTY TIP

Try this recipe with maple syrup instead of brown sugar: use 1-1/5 cups (300 ml) maple syrup and 1-1/5 cups (300 ml) 35% cream. Bring to a boil and let simmer for 4 minutes.

DID YOU KNOW?

Pudding chômeur, which literally means "unemployment pudding" or "poor man's pudding," is a traditional dessert from the French-speaking province of Quebec, in Canada. It was concocted during the Great Depression by female factory workers using common, inexpensive ingredients like flour, water, and maple syrup (a Quebec staple).

FOR SAUCE

2 cups (460 g) brown sugar, lightly packed
1 cup (250 ml) water
2 tbsp (30 g) butter

FOR BATTER

2 cups (290 g) flour
2 tsp (8 g) baking powder
1 pinch salt
1/2 cup (115 g) unsalted butter, softened
1 cup (200 g) sugar
2 eggs
1/2 cup (125 ml) milk

PREPARATION

Preheat oven to 375°F (190°C).

For sauce: In a pot, bring brown sugar, water, and butter to a boil. Let simmer for 4 minutes. Set aside.

For batter: In a bowl, sift together flour, baking powder, and salt. Set aside.

In another bowl, and using an electric hand or stand mixer, cream together butter and sugar. Add eggs one at a time, mixing well after each addition. Alternately add dry ingredients and milk; don't overmix. Pour batter into a baking pan and then pour sauce over top. Bake for 45 minutes, or until a toothpick inserted into the center comes out clean.

44

MACARONS

MAKES 30 MACARONS
PREP TIME: 1 HOUR AND 45 MINUTES

REST TIME: 3 HOURS

TASTY TIP

To make homemade raspberry purée, crush 2 cups (260 g) fresh or frozen raspberries and then strain with a wire mesh strainer to remove the seeds.

FOR COOKIES

3/4 cup (150 g) sugar
1/4 cup (60 ml) water
4 egg whites, divided between 2 bowls
1-1/2 cups (150 g) almond flour
1-1/4 cups (150 g) icing sugar
Red food coloring

FOR RASPBERRY FILLING

1/3 cup (65 g) sugar
1/4 tsp (1 g) cornstarch
1 egg
1/4 cup (60 ml) store-bought or homemade raspberry purée
1/3 cup (80 g) unsalted butter, softened
Fresh raspberries

PREPARATION

For cookies: Preheat oven to 350°F (175°C).

In a pot, heat sugar and water together until the temperature reaches 250°F (120°C).

Meanwhile, using a hand or stand mixer with the whisk attachment, beat 2 egg whites until frothy. When the sugar and water has reached the right temperature, slowly pour the mixture into the egg whites, whipping constantly. Continue beating at medium speed until the mixture is cool.

While the egg white mixture is beating, mix together almond flour and icing sugar in a bowl. Add remaining egg whites and food coloring and mix well. Using a flexible plastic spatula, fold in 1/3 of the egg white, sugar, and water mixture and mix well. Fold in remaining egg white mixture.

Transfer batter to a pastry bag with a round tip. Pipe out 1-1/2-inch rounds onto a baking sheet lined with parchment paper or a silicone baking mat. Allow to dry, uncovered, until cookies are no longer sticky to the touch. Bake for 8 to 10 minutes.

For raspberry filling: In a pot, heat sugar, cornstarch, egg, and raspberry purée over low heat, whisking constantly. Let simmer for 2 minutes to allow filling to thicken, and then remove from heat. Let the mixture cool to 140°F (60°C) and then add butter, whisking constantly.

Top half of the cookies with a bit of filling and fresh raspberry halves. Close with remaining cookies to make small sandwiches and then refrigerate macarons for at least 3 hours.

45

LUSCIOUS LEMON CREAM CUPS

SERVES 6
PREP TIME: 30 MINUTES

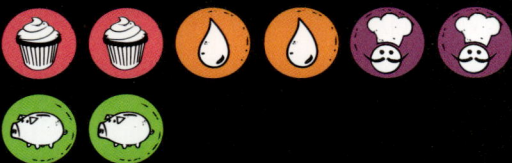

REST TIME: 3 HOURS

FOR LEMON CREAM

1 cup (250 ml) lemon juice
2/3 cup plus 2 tbsp (150 g) sugar
5 eggs
Zest of 1/2 lemon
1 gelatin sheet, softened according to package directions
1/2 cup plus 1 tbsp (130 g) cold unsalted butter

Fresh strawberries, washed, hulled, and halved
Sliced almonds (for garnish)

FOR SYRUP

2/5 cup (100 ml) water
2/5 cup (100 ml) honey

PREPARATION

For lemon cream: In a pot, over medium heat, cook lemon juice, sugar, eggs, and lemon zest, whisking constantly. As soon as the mixture starts to bubble, remove from heat and strain with a fine wire mesh strainer. Stir in gelatin and butter. Divide cream equally between 6 serving glasses and chill for at least 3 hours.

For syrup: Bring water and honey to a boil and cook for 2 minutes. Refrigerate.

Garnish each cup with a few strawberries and a sprinkling of sliced almonds, drizzle with syrup, and serve.

TASTY TIP

For extra crunch, sprinkle a small handful of granola or homemade muesli over top of each serving.

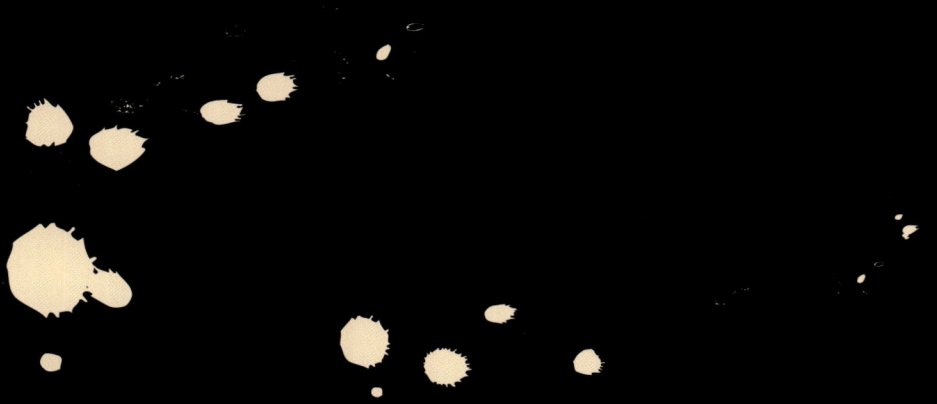

46

WHITE CHOCOLATE MACADAMIA COOKIES

MAKES 16 COOKIES
PREP TIME: 30 MINUTES

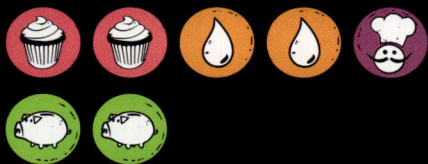

INGREDIENTS

1 cup (150 g) flour, sifted
1/4 tsp (1 g) baking powder
1/2 tsp (3 g) salt
6 tbsp (85 g) unsalted butter, softened
3/4 cup plus 1 tbsp (180 g) brown sugar, lightly packed
1 egg
2/3 cup (90 g) macadamia nuts, chopped
4/5 cup (150 g) white chocolate, chopped

PREPARATION

Preheat oven to 350°F (175°C).

In a bowl, combine flour, baking powder, and salt. Set aside.

In another bowl, cream together butter and brown sugar. Add egg. Add dry ingredients, nuts, and chocolate, and mix to combine; don't overmix.

Using spoons, form dough into small balls (about 2 tbsp each) and drop onto a baking sheet lined with parchment paper, or a silicone baking mat.

Bake for 10 minutes. Cookies should be soft in the center and lightly golden around the edges.

47

THE TARTE TATIN

SERVES 8
PREP TIME: 1 HOUR AND 30 MINUTES

INGREDIENTS

1/2 package (about 1/2 lb) store-bought puff pastry
2/3 cup (120 g) sugar
3 tbsp (45 ml) water
1/4 cup (55 g) unsalted butter
8 baking apples (Lobo, Cortland, etc.), cored, peeled, and halved
1 tsp (5 ml) lemon juice

PREPARATION

Preheat oven to 400°F (200°C).

Roll out puff pastry dough into a circle, about 1/8 inch thick and the same diameter as the pie pan (10 inches). Pierce pastry a few times with a fork. Transfer to a plate and refrigerate.

Meanwhile, in a pot, heat sugar and water over medium-high heat until light brown in color. Remove from heat and add butter, stirring with a wooden spoon. Pour evenly into the pie pan. Arrange apples in tightly-packed rows over the caramel and pour lemon juice over apples.

Bake for 20 minutes. After 20 minutes, cover apples with rolled-out puff pastry dough and bake for 30 minutes longer. Remove from oven and let sit for 5 minutes before carefully flipping onto a serving plate. Serve.

DID YOU KNOW?

The world's largest *tarte tatin* was made in 1998 by a French pastry chef named Claude Bisson, and measured over 8 feet!

48

GRILLED CHOCOLATE BANANAS

SERVES 2
PREP TIME: 1 HOUR

INGREDIENTS

2 ripe bananas
1/4 cup (46 g) chocolate of your choice, roughly chopped

PREPARATION

Make this deliciously simple dessert to finish off a barbecue dinner!

While your meal is cooking on the barbecue, take bananas and, using a small knife, slice down the entire length of each banana, cutting through just to the flesh. Put chocolate into the opening of each banana.

Wrap bananas in aluminum foil. When your food has finished cooking, turn off barbecue and place bananas on hot grill. Close barbecue, but don't turn it back on.

To serve, just peel the bananas and eat right out of the peel, or scoop into dessert dishes and top with ice cream!

RUM BABAS

49

SERVES 6
PREP TIME: 1 HOUR

REST TIME: 2 HOURS

TASTY TIP

If you don't have a stand mixer, give your arms a good workout by kneading the dough by hand!

FOR BABAS

1 cup (150 g) flour
2 tsp (10 g) fresh active yeast (also called compressed or cake yeast)
1/3 cup plus 2 tbsp (100 g) unsalted butter, softened
1/2 tsp (2 g) salt
1 tbsp (15 g) sugar
2 eggs

FOR RUM SYRUP

3 cups (750 ml) water
1-1/2 cups (500 g) sugar
Zest of 1 lemon
Zest of 1 orange
1 vanilla bean, halved, seeds scraped out and reserved
1/2 cup (125 ml) rum

FOR WHIPPED CREAM

1 cup (250 ml) 35% cream
1/4 cup (25 g) icing sugar, sifted

PREPARATION

For babas: Using a stand mixer with the dough hook attachment, mix together all ingredients for 5 minutes, until batter is smooth. Remove from bowl and shape into a ball. Lightly flour a clean bowl. Transfer dough to bowl, cover, and let sit in a warm place for 1 hour.

Meanwhile, butter 6 rum baba molds, or cup-shaped molds, and set aside. Preheat oven to 350°F (175°C).

Divide dough into 6 equal portions and shape into balls. Place in buttered molds. Cover with a tea towel and let sit in a warm place, until dough rises up to the edges of the molds. Bake for 25 minutes, let cool, and remove from molds.

For rum syrup: In a pot, bring all ingredients to a boil, except rum. Remove from heat, let cool, and then add rum.

For whipped cream: Using a hand or stand mixer, whip cream and icing sugar until stiff peaks form.

To finish, heat syrup, but don't let it boil. Dip each rum baba in the syrup for 10 to 15 seconds and let them drain on a baking rack for 1 minute. Serve with whipped cream.

50

THE ICE CREAM SANDWICH

MAKES 18 SANDWICHES
PREP TIME: 1 HOUR

REST TIME: 30 MINUTES

INGREDIENTS

1-1/3 cups plus 2 tbsp (350 g) unsalted butter, softened
2 cups (215 g) icing sugar
1/4 tsp (1 g) salt
2-1/3 cups (340 g) flour
1 cup (90 g) cocoa powder
1/4 tsp (1 g) baking powder
1 carton store-bought ice cream of your choice
(vanilla, chocolate, butterscotch, etc.)

PREPARATION

Preheat oven to 350°F (175°C).

In a bowl, cream together butter, icing sugar, and salt. Add flour, cocoa powder, and baking powder, and mix until smooth; don't overmix. Wrap in plastic wrap and refrigerate for 30 minutes.

Lightly flour a flat work surface. Using a rolling pin, roll out dough to a little less than 1/4 inch thick (about 4 mm). With a knife, cut dough into rectangles, about 2-1/2 inches x 3-1/2 inches each. Transfer to a baking sheet lined with parchment paper, or a silicone baking mat. Refrigerate for 15 minutes.

Bake for 8 minutes and then let cool completely.

To assemble sandwiches, remove ice cream from carton and, using a knife, cut into 1/2-inch slices. Cut each slice into 2 equal pieces. Sandwich each piece of ice cream between two cookies. Store in the freezer in an airtight container.

TASTY TIP

Ice cream sandwiches don't always have to be vanilla! Double the intensity with chocolate ice cream, create peanut butter cup-style delights, or pack a triple punch with Neapolitan ice cream!

51

BISCOTTI & AFFOGATO

MAKES 20 BISCOTTI
PREP TIME: 1 HOUR

FOR BISCOTTI

1/3 cup plus 1 tsp (85 g) unsalted butter, softened
2/3 cup (140 g) sugar
1/4 tsp (1 g) salt
Zest of 1 lemon
2 eggs
2 cups (300 g) flour
1 tsp (5 g) baking powder
2/5 cup plus 1 tbsp (60 g) shelled pistachios
3/4 cup plus 1 tbsp (60 g) dried fruit of your choice
(figs, cranberries, apricots, etc.)

FOR AFFOGATO

1 scoop vanilla ice cream
1 oz liqueur of your choice
(Baileys Irish Cream, Calvados, amaretto, Frangelico, etc.)
1 shot freshly brewed espresso

PREPARATION

For biscotti: Preheat oven to 350°F (175°C).

Cream together butter, sugar, salt, and lemon zest. Add eggs one at a time, mixing well after each addition. Add flour, baking powder, pistachios, and dried fruit. Mix just to combine; don't overmix.

On a baking sheet covered in parchment paper, or a silicone baking mat, shape dough into a 5-inch x 8-inch rectangle.

Bake for 30 minutes, and then let cool completely. Using a serrated knife, cut log into 1/2-inch slices. Transfer sliced biscotti back to the baking sheet and bake for 3 minutes at the same temperature, flip, and bake for 3 minutes longer.

Drop a scoop of vanilla ice cream into a small coffee cup or glass. Serve the cup on a saucer or a small plate with a biscotti, a shot of liqueur, and a shot of espresso on the side. Pour hot espresso over ice cream right before serving.

DID YOU KNOW?

Before it arrived in Europe in the 17th century, coffee was brewed and consumed in Arabia and Yemen as a cure for many illnesses (particularly stomach ailments), often in the morning, much like today's coffee drinkers.

52

ROASTED PEACHES

SERVES 6
PREP TIME: 30 MINUTES

INGREDIENTS

1 tsp (5 g) fresh ginger, peeled and chopped
Juice of 1 lemon
1/4 cup (60 ml) honey
1/2 cup (125 ml) water
1 vanilla bean, halved, seeds scraped out and reserved
3 ripe peaches, halved and pitted
1 cup (130 g) fresh raspberries

PREPARATION

Preheat oven to 400°F (200°C).

In an oven-safe pan or skillet, bring ginger, lemon juice, honey, water, and vanilla bean pod and seeds to a boil. Arrange peaches in the pan, cut side up. Cook in the oven for 10 minutes, drizzling peaches every few minutes with the syrup at the bottom of the pan. After 10 minutes, add raspberries and roast for another 8 minutes, until peaches are tender.

Serve with vanilla ice cream or crème fraîche.

TASTY TIP

Top a simple cake with roasted peaches to add a gourmet touch!

53

COFFEE PANNA COTTA

SERVES 4
PREP TIME: 1 HOUR

REST TIME: 6 HOURS

INGREDIENTS

2 gelatin sheets, softened accorded to package directions
1 cup (250 ml) 35% cream
1/4 cup (60 ml) milk
4 tsp (8 g) ground coffee
8 tsp (35 g) sugar
1/2 cup (65 g) milk chocolate, roughly chopped
1/3 cup plus 1 tbsp (95 ml) sour cream

PREPARATION

In a pot, bring cream and milk to a boil. When mixture starts to bubble, remove from heat and add coffee. Cover and let infuse for 8 minutes. Strain using a fine wire mesh sieve.

Bring infused cream and milk to a boil with the sugar. When mixture starts to bubble, remove from heat and add softened gelatin. Mix well, making sure gelatin is completely dissolved. In a bowl, pour this mixture over the chopped chocolate. Let sit for 2 minutes and then mix together with a whisk. Add sour cream and mix well. Pour into small individual bowls or glasses and refrigerate for at least 6 hours before serving.

DID YOU KNOW?

Early panna cotta recipes didn't contain gelatin; instead, they included a step in which fish bones were boiled to extract the collagen, which turns to gelatin!

Gelatin is actually an animal by-product, which is why many vegetarians (and all vegans!) choose not to eat foods or use products containing the substance. Popular alternatives include agar-agar (derived from seaweed), pectin, and carrageenan.

Yule Log

54

SERVES 10
PREP TIME: 2 HOURS AND 35 MINUTES

DID YOU KNOW?

Originally, Yule logs were entire trees, burned to celebrate the winter solstice, and as a part of traditional Yule or Christmas celebrations. It was often sprinkled with oil, salt, and mulled wine and then blessed with a prayer before being lit.

FOR CAKE

4 egg yolks
3 eggs
2/3 cup (135 g) sugar
4 egg whites
3 tbsp (40 g) sugar
1/2 cup (80 g) flour, sifted

FOR SYRUP

2/5 cup (100 ml) water
2/5 cup (85 g) sugar
1 oz (28 ml) kirsch or rum

FOR GARNISH

1 recipe pastry cream (see recipe on page 108)
2 cups (260 g) fresh or frozen raspberries
1 recipe meringue (see recipe on page 062)

PREPARATION

For cake: Preheat oven to 350°F (175°C).

Using a hand or stand mixer with the whisk attachment, beat egg yolks, eggs, and 2/3 cup sugar on medium speed for 8 minutes, and then set aside. Using the mixer, whip egg whites, gradually sprinkling in the 3 tbsp sugar, until soft peaks form.

In a bowl, and using a flexible rubber spatula, gently fold the two mixtures together. Fold in flour. Pour batter into a jelly roll pan lined with parchment paper, or a silicone baking mat. Bake for 10 minutes, just until the top feels springy to the touch. Cover with a tea towel and let cool completely.

For syrup: In a pot, bring water and sugar to a boil. Let boil for 3 minutes, remove from heat, and add alcohol. Chill in the refrigerator.

To assemble cake: Turn cake onto a tea towel, with the longest side facing you. Carefully remove parchment paper. Brush cake with syrup and then, using an offset baker's spatula, spread pastry cream evenly over entire surface of cake. Using the tea towel as a guide, carefully roll up into a log, starting with the edge closest to you. Slice off both ends. Using an offset spatula, frost entire log with meringue, spreading it from one end to the other. Use a kitchen torch to lightly brown the top. Serve.

55

CRÊPES

MAKES 12 CRÊPES
PREP TIME: 20 MINUTES

REST TIME: 1 HOUR

INGREDIENTS

1-2/3 cups (250 g) flour
3/4 cup plus 2 tbsp (175 g) sugar
1 pinch salt
4 eggs
3/4 cup plus 1/2 tbsp (187 ml) water
1-1/2 cups (375 ml) milk
1/4 cup (55 ml) unsalted butter, melted

PREPARATION

In a bowl, combine flour, sugar, and salt.

In another bowl, whisk together eggs, water, and milk. Pour into flour mixture and whisk thoroughly. Add butter. Strain with a fine wire mesh strainer. Cover and refrigerate batter for at least 1 hour, overnight if possible.

Heat a pan over medium heat. Melt a bit of butter and, using a ladle, pour about 1/4 cup (60 ml) of batter into the center of the pan, swirling pan to coat. Cook until bottom is golden brown, flip, and cook until golden brown.

Slide crêpe out of pan, add a bit more butter, and repeat with remaining batter. Top with maple syrup or toppings of your choice.

DID YOU KNOW?

In Brittany, France, a popular street food is *galette saucisse*, fresh grilled sausage wrapped in a buckwheat crêpe and served from market carts.

56

NANAIMO BARS

MAKES 16 BARS
PREP TIME: 1 HOUR

DID YOU KNOW?

The Nanaimo bar is a Canadian dessert, named after the city in which it was invented: Nanaimo, British Columbia. They were invented by Mabel Jenkins in the 1950s, and were originally called Mabel bars.

FOR COOKIE BASE

1/2 cup (115 g) unsalted butter
1/4 cup (57 g) brown sugar, lightly packed
1/2 cup (60 g) dark chocolate, roughly chopped
1 egg, beaten
2 cups (160 g) social tea cookies, crushed
1 cup (78 g) shredded unsweetened coconut
1/2 cup (75 g) walnuts, chopped

FOR FILLING

1/4 cup (55 g) unsalted butter, softened
2 tbsp (30 ml) 35% cream
2 tbsp (20 g) custard powder
2 cups (254 g) icing sugar
1 tsp (5 ml) vanilla extract

FOR CHOCOLATE TOPPING

2/3 cup (80 g) dark chocolate, roughly chopped
1 tbsp (15 g) unsalted butter

PREPARATION

Butter a 9-inch baking pan and line with parchment paper. Set aside.

For cookie base: In a pot, heat butter, brown sugar, and chocolate. When butter is melted, add egg, whisking constantly until mixture becomes thick. Remove from heat and stir in crushed cookies, coconut, and walnuts. Transfer to the prepared baking pan and press into an even layer. Refrigerate until cold.

For filling: Whisk together all ingredients. Spread evenly over chilled cookie base. Refrigerate until filling is firm.

For topping: Melt chocolate and butter in a bain-marie. Spread evenly over filling and refrigerate until set.

Cut into 16 squares and serve.

57

CARAMEL BANANA CRUNCH PUDDING

SERVES 8
PREP TIME: 35 MINUTES

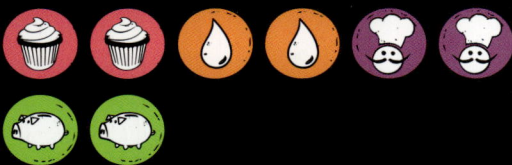

REST TIME: 6 HOURS

TASTY TIP

For a quicker version of this crunchy topping, combine crumbled store-bought sponge toffee and salted peanuts.

DID YOU KNOW?

Synchronized swimmers use gelatin to keep their hair in place during competitions!

FOR BANANA COMPOTE

4 bananas, cut into rounds
6 tbsp (80 g) brown sugar
2 tsp (10 ml) lemon juice

FOR CRÈME CARAMEL

3/4 cup plus 2 tsp (160 g) sugar
1/3 cup (80 ml) water
2 cups (500 ml) 35% cream, hot
8 egg yolks
3 tbsp (45 g) sugar
2 gelatin sheets, softened accorded to package directions

FOR PEANUT BRITTLE

1/3 cup (66 g) sugar
1/4 cup plus 1 tsp (65 ml) corn syrup
3/5 cup plus 1 tsp (94 g) roasted salted peanuts
1/4 tsp (1 g) baking soda

PREPARATION

For banana compote: In a pan, cook all ingredients over high heat, until bananas are cooked through. Add a bit of water as needed.

For crème caramel: In a pot, bring 3/4 cup plus 2 tsp sugar, and water, to a boil. Cook until the mixture turns a dark golden brown. Add hot cream in a slow, steady stream, whisking constantly, to make a caramel. Be very careful during this step, as the hot mixture may splatter.

In a bowl, whisk together egg yolks and 3 tbsp sugar. Add 1/3 of the caramel, mix well, and then add this mixture to the pot with the remaining caramel. Cook over medium heat, stirring constantly with a wooden spoon, until the mixture is thick enough to coat the back of the spoon. Remove from heat, add softened gelatin, and stir. Pour into glasses or serving bowls and chill for at least 6 hours.

For peanut brittle: In a pot, bring sugar and corn syrup to a boil. Cook until the mixture reaches 320°F (160°C). Stir in peanuts and then add baking soda—the mixture will immediately start to become frothy. Spread mixture evenly over a baking sheet lined with parchment paper, or a silicone baking mat. Allow to set and then, using a knife, crack into pieces.

Right before serving, garnish each dish with banana compote and peanut brittle.

58

CITRUS SURPRISE

SERVES 6
PREP TIME: 45 MINUTES

FOR SYRUP

1/3 cup (80 ml) honey
1/3 cup (80 ml) water
1 tbsp (15 ml) hazelnut oil

FOR FRUIT

2 pink grapefruits
1 orange
1 blood orange
5 medjool dates, pitted and cut into thin strips
Seeds from 1/2 pomegranate

PREPARATION

For syrup: In a pot, bring honey and water to a boil. Let simmer for 3 minutes, remove from heat, and refrigerate until cool. Add hazelnut oil to cooled syrup.

Using a sharp knife, peel and segment citrus fruits, making sure to remove the pith and membranes. Transfer to a salad bowl. Add dates and pomegranate seeds. Pour syrup over all, mix well, and serve in pretty glasses.

DID YOU KNOW?

The grapefruit only became a commercial success in 1929, when the red, or pink, grapefruit was introduced.

59

BREAD PUDDING & APPLE BUTTER

MAKES 10 SERVINGS
PREP TIME: 1 HOUR AND 15 MINUTES

REST TIME: 1 HOUR

DID YOU KNOW?

Many countries have their own versions of bread pudding. This dessert is especially popular in Cuba, Ireland, Great Britain, France, Belgium, Argentina, and the United States.

FOR BREAD PUDDING

1-1/2 cups (375 ml) cups milk
1/4 cup (50 g) fresh ginger, peeled and finely chopped
12 cups (680 g) day-old white bread, cut into 1-inch cubes
5 eggs
3/4 cup (150 g) sugar
2 cups (500 ml) 35% cream
1/3 cup (80 ml) brandy
1/4 cup (100 g) candied ginger, finely diced

FOR APPLE BUTTER

4 red apples, cored and diced
1/3 cup (75 g) unsalted butter
3 tbsp (42 g) brown sugar
1 tsp (5 ml) vanilla extract

PREPARATION

In a pot, heat milk. When milk starts to bubble, remove from heat and add fresh ginger. Cover and let infuse for 30 minutes, and then strain with a fine wire mesh strainer. Discard ginger.

In a bowl, whisk together eggs and sugar. Add infused milk, cream, and brandy, and mix well. Place bread in a large bowl and pour milk mixture over top. Add candied ginger and toss gently to coat bread. Cover and refrigerate for 1 hour.

To make apple butter, preheat oven to 325°F (160°C). Place apples in a baking dish and bake for 15 minutes, or until tender, stirring occasionally.

While apples are still hot, purée in a food processor until smooth and then strain using a fine wire mesh strainer. Add butter, brown sugar, and vanilla extract and mix well using a whisk, making sure brown sugar is dissolved and butter is completely melted. Cover and chill in the refrigerator.

Preheat oven to 350°F (175°C). Butter an 8-inch x 10-inch baking pan. Evenly spread bread mixture at the bottom of the pan and bake for 40 minutes, or until bread is golden brown.

Serve bread pudding with a dollop of apple butter.

60

CHOCOLATE POTS DE CRÈME

SERVES 4
PREP TIME: 30 MINUTES

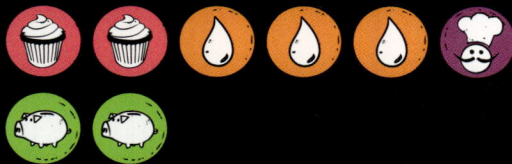

REST TIME: 3 HOURS

INGREDIENTS

1 cup (250 ml) 15% cream
4 egg yolks
2 tbsp (25 g) sugar
3/4 cup (150 g) dark chocolate pastilles or dark chocolate, roughly chopped

PREPARATION

In a pot, heat cream. Set aside.

In a bowl, whisk together egg yolks and sugar. Pour a bit of hot cream into the egg yolk mixture, whisking constantly, and then pour this mixture into the pot with the cream.

Cook over medium heat, stirring constantly with a wooden spoon, until the mixture is thick enough to coat the back of the spoon and reaches a temperature of 180°F (82°C). In a bowl, pour this mixture over the chocolate and whisk until smooth.

Pour into individual teacups or glasses and refrigerate for at least 3 hours before serving.

TASTY TIP

Garnish with whipped cream, toasted nuts, or fresh berries.

INGREDIENTS INDEX

A

ALCOHOL 152
ALMOND EXTRACT 058
ALMOND POWDER 058, 084, 134
ALMONDS 086, 096, 122, 136
APPLE 072, 142, 170

B

BAKING POWDER 034, 044,
.... 052, 080, 094, 116, 124, 132, 140, 148, 152
BAKING SODA 048, 166
BANANA 076, 094, 144, 166
BASIL 118
BLACK PEPPER 084
BLUEBERRIES 092, 104
BOURBON 100
BRANDY 170
BREAD 170
BROWN SUGAR 034, 046, 052, 070,
.... 072, 080, 094, 100, 104, 112, 132, 140, 164, 166, 170
BUTTERMILK 048, 116

C

CARROTS 052
CASHEW BUTTER 092
CHERRIES 064, 088
CHOCOLATE, DARK ... 032, 060, 074, 080, 120, 130, 144, 164, 172
CHOCOLATE, MILK 060, 074, 080, 130, 144, 156
CHOCOLATE, WHITE 140
CINNAMON 046, 050, 052, 070, 072, 094, 096, 104, 106
CLOVE 046
COCOA 048, 080, 110, 148

COCONUT..040, 164
COFFEE...110, 152, 156
CORN SYRUP............................088, 100, 112, 166
CORNSTARCH..........................050, 072, 108, 134
CRANBERRIES...038, 056
CREAM CHEESE 036, 048, 092
CREAM, 15%...172
CREAM, 35% 032, 038, 046, 064, 068, 070, 074, 086,
...................088, 092, 094, 124, 130, 146, 156, 164, 166, 170
CUSTARD POWDER...164

D

DARK BEER...088
DATES..056, 094, 168
DRIED FRUIT..152

E

EARL GREY TEA 074

F

FIGS...034, 116
FOOD COLORING..048, 134
FRESH ACTIVE YEAST 106, 146

G

GELATIN 136, 156, 166
GINGER.............................046, 070, 076, 154, 170
GINGER, CANDIED 170
GOLDEN RAISINS 056, 116
GRAHAM CRACKERS...........................036, 092, 128

GRAPESEED OIL 052

H

HAZELNUT OIL...168
HAZELNUT PRALINE.......................................122
HONEY.......................082, 086, 092, 096, 136, 154, 168

I

ICE CREAM...148, 152
ICING SUGAR 027, 044, 048, 050, 062,
...........................122, 124, 130, 134, 146, 148, 164

K

KIRSCH..064, 158

L

LADYFINGER COOKIES.....................................110
LEMON 036, 038, 044, 050, 062, 084, 104,
.........................116, 118, 124, 136, 142, 146, 152, 154, 166
LIME 076, 128

M

MANGO...082
MAPLE SYRUP.......................................052, 160
MASCARPONE CHEESE 048, 052, 110
MILK.........................027, 032, 050, 060, 068, 074, 082, 088,
.........................098, 106, 108, 116, 122, 132, 156, 160, 170
MILK, EVAPORATED.......................................112
MILK, SWEETENED CONDENSED....................098, 128
MOLASSES...088

N

NUTMEG 046, 070, 094
NUTS, CASHEW 092
NUTS, MACADAMIA 140
NUTS, PECANS 036, 056, 092, 100, 104
NUTS, PISTACHIO 086, 096, 152
NUTS, WALNUTS 056, 096, 164

O

ORANGE 070, 074, 076, 082, 096, 146, 168
ORANGE, BLOOD 168
ORANGE, CANDIED 056, 086
ORANGE LIQUEUR 074

P

PEACH 104, 154
PEANUTS, ROASTED SALTED 166
PEAR 084
PHYLLO PASTRY 096
PINEAPPLE 076
PINK GRAPEFRUIT 168
POMEGRANATE 168
PRUNES 056
PUFF PASTRY 050, 058, 130, 142
PUMPKIN 046, 070

R

RASPBERRIES 130, 134, 154, 158
RASPBERRY PURÉE 134
RED WINE 070
RICOTTA CHEESE 070
ROLLED (OLD-FASHIONED) OATS 034, 104
RUM 056, 074, 146, 158

S

SEA SALT 088
SOCIAL TEA COOKIES 164
SOUR CREAM 044, 064, 092, 156
SPARKLING WINE 082, 118
STAR ANISE 084
STRAWBERRIES 036, 118, 124, 136

V

VANILLA BEAN 044, 052, 068,
.... 070, 076, 084, 092, 100, 110, 146, 154
VANILLA EXTRACT 034, 040, 048, 112, 164, 170
VEGETABLE OIL 098, 106
VINEGAR 048

W

WATERMELON 082
WHIPPED CREAM 128, 130, 146

Y

YOGURT 038, 082

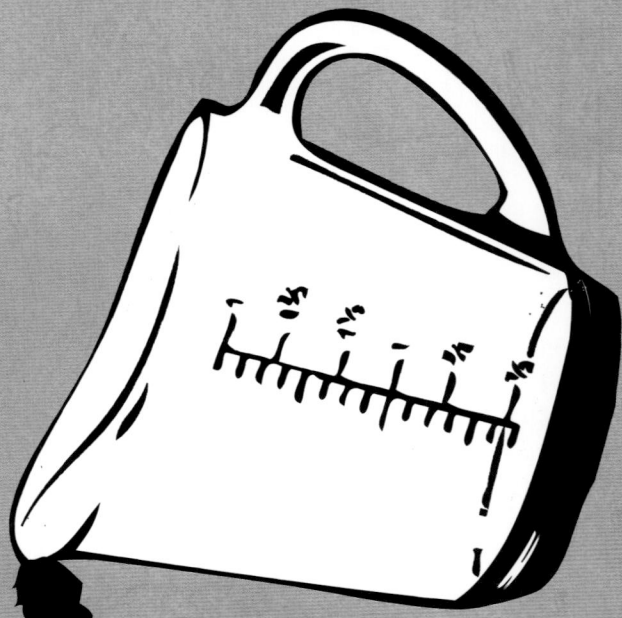

CONVERSION CHART

```
1 dl ...................... 10 cl ...................... 100 ml
1 tbsp .................................................. 15 ml
1 tsp .................................................... 5 ml
1 oz .................... 30 ml
1 cup ................... 250 ml
4 cup ................... 1 l
1/2 cup ................ 125 ml
1/3 cup ................ 80 ml
2/3 cup ................ 160 ml
1/4 cup ................ 60 ml
3/4 cup ................ 180 ml
1/5 cup ................ 50 ml
2/5 cup ................ 100 ml
3/5 cup ................ 150 ml
4/5 cup ................ 200 ml
1 lb ..................... 450 g
2 lbs .................... 900 g
2.2 lbs ................. 1 kg
400°F ................... 200°C ..................... T/7
350°F ................... 175°C ..................... T/6
300°F ................... 150°C ..................... T/5
```

NOTES

THE WORLD'S 60 BEST

SALADS
PERIOD.

THE WORLD'S 60 BEST

PASTA SAUCES
PERIOD.

THE WORLD'S 60 BEST

BURGERS
PERIOD.

THE WORLD'S 60 BEST

LUNCHES
PERIOD.

THE WORLD'S 60 BEST

RECIPES FOR STUDENTS
PERIOD.

THE WORLD'S 60 BEST

PIZZAS
PERIOD.

THE WORLD'S 60 BEST

GRATINS
PERIOD.

THE WORLD'S 60 BEST

STUFFED DISHES
PERIOD.

HEALTHY SMOOTHIES
PERIOD.

SOUPS
PERIOD.

STEWS
PERIOD.

ROAST DISHES
PERIOD.